ON DYING WELL

GS Misc 600

ON DYING WELL

A Contribution
to the Euthanasia Debate

Second Edition

CHURCH HOUSE
PUBLISHING

Church House Publishing
Church House
Great Smith Street
London
SW1P 3NZ

ISBN 0 7151 6587 9 2nd edition
(ISBN 0 7151 6539 9 1st edition)

First published 1975
Reprinted 1975
Second edition 2000

Published 2000 for the Board for Social Responsibility
of the Church of England by Church House Publishing.

First edition copyright © The Central Board of Finance
of the Church of England 1975

Second edition copyright © The Archbishops' Council 1975, 2000

This report has only the authority of the Working Party who produced it. It has been approved by the Board for Social Responsibility.

Acknowledgement: The publisher gratefully acknowledges permission from the Voluntary Euthanasia Society to reproduce material (pp. 2, 3).

Cover design by ADPS Ltd

Printed in England by Halstan & Co. Ltd

Contents

Members of the Working Party

The Revd M. A. H. Melinsky, MA, Chairman of the Working Party; Chief Secretary of the Advisory Council for the Church's Ministry; Honorary Canon of Norwich Cathedral, and Chairman of the Institute of Religion and Medicine

The Lord Amulree, MD, FRCP, Consulting Physician, University College Hospital; Former President of the British Geriatric Society

The Revd P. R. Baelz, MA, BD, Canon of Christ Church and Regius Professor of Moral and Pastoral Theology in the University of Oxford

R. M. Hare, MA, FBA, White's Professor of Moral Philosophy and Fellow of Corpus Christi College, Oxford.

B. G. Mitchell, MA, Nolloth Professor of the Philosophy of the Christian Religion, and Fellow of Oriel College, Oxford

The Worshipful and Revd E. Garth Moore, MA, Barrister-at-law; Chancellor of the Dioceses of Durham, Southwark and Gloucester; Fellow of Corpus Christi College, Cambridge, and Vicar of the Guild Church of St Mary Abchurch, London

Dr Cicely Saunders, OBE, MA, FRCP, SRN, AIMSW, Medical Director of St Christopher's Hospice, Sydenham, London

Contributors to the second edition

The Revd Michael Banner, F.D. Maurice Professor of Moral and Social Theology, King's College, London

J. S. Horner, Visiting Professor of Medical Ethics at University of Central Lancashire

H. McQuay, Professor of Pain Relief, Churchill Hospital, Oxford; Fellow of Balliol College, Oxford

J. R. Montgomery, Reader in Health Care Law, University of Southampton

Pat Walsh, Senior Lecturer in Medical Ethics, the Centre of Medical Law and Ethics, King's College, London

Preface to the Second Edition

On Dying Well was first produced in 1974. It has been out of print for many years and, in response to numerous requests, the Board for Social Responsibility has decided to reprint it in full because it contains material that is still relevant in the current debate over euthanasia. This is a tribute to the members of the original Working Party who researched and wrote the Report. Their individual contributions to the theory and practice of care of the terminally ill have continued to be of importance in the years since they met. The Report's lasting value is a reflection of their wisdom and understanding.

Most of the Report has been reprinted unchanged, but some important additions and changes have been made where necessary. The Board for Social Responsibility asked Professor Stuart Horner to provide a new Introduction, which locates *On Dying Well* in its historical context and identifies some of the key issues as the debate has developed. Professor Horner served with distinction as Chairman of the British Medical Association's Ethics Committee from 1989 to 1997. He is a member of the Board's Science, Medicine and Technology Committee but he has written his Introduction in a purely personal capacity. Chapter 6, which deals with legal issues, has been redrafted by Jonathan Montgomery to take account of cases since 1974 that have a bearing on the subject. Professor Henry McQuay, a consultant in pain relief, has commented upon the Report's medical references. Pat Walsh, Professor Michael Banner and Dame Cicely Saunders have added a comprehensive list of books and articles published since 1974 to the Bibliography. Finally, there is a new appendix, which consists of the Joint Submission to the House of Lords Select Committee on Medical Ethics produced in 1993 by the House of Bishops of the Church of England and the Roman Catholic Bishops' Conference of England and Wales.

I should like to express my gratitude to those who have contributed to the new edition of the Report, as well as to the original Working Party members. I am delighted that *On Dying Well* is once again available to those who wish to see how the Church of England has contributed to the debate about euthanasia.

✠ *Richard Oxon:*
Chairman, Board for Social Responsibility

Twenty-five Years On:
Introduction to the Second Edition

Professor J Stuart Horner

The decision of the Board for Social Responsibility to reissue with little amendment its booklet on euthanasia, first published twenty-five years ago, will no doubt confirm to its critics that the Church of England is locked into a frozen past. Surely the arguments have changed? In fact they have not. Anyone who troubles to read the document will find it as relevant to today's debate as it was when the Working Party first met. Of course events have moved on. Nowadays the report would use inclusive language and not appear to assume that only men faced these dilemmas. Some of the language and presentation is admittedly dated but the principles are unchanged.

Probably the most significant change has been the terminology. The Working Party clearly struggled with the limitations that concepts such as *active euthanasia* and *passive euthanasia* imposed upon the debate. Table 1 on p.x shows a more comprehensive taxonomy of the medical decisions available at the end of life. Each possible decision except the first may be taken either with, or without, the specific informed consent of the patient. It is unfortunate that debates on the subject, particularly in the media, wander confusingly from one to the other, when the medical and philosophical implications are profoundly different. Most decisions require careful clinical judgement and frequently cause great-heart searching within the health care team, in order to determine precisely in which category the decision falls. Ultimately no outside observer can judge the intentions or motives of those involved and the true character of the decision is easily concealed. For this reason it is essential that the whole health care team, as well as the relatives, is involved in the discussions.

Since the Working Party reported, society has moved further down the road of individual autonomy and choice, often expressed in a language of rights. Yet the Working Party addressed even this issue. On page 20 it explored the relationship between self-determination and trust in God. Most churches would now approve the language of human rights, based on the 'dignity' of human beings made in the image of God. Christians would wish all people to enjoy the freedom to make their own decisions, not least in the field of health care. They reject however an unbridled autonomy which ignores the moral claims of others, or their own ultimate accountability to God. The primacy of individual autonomy is yet one more manifestation of the idolatry to which humankind is subject. A further development since the Working Party's document has been a change in medical and legal practice in The Netherlands, the effects of which were assessed in a ground-breaking study.[1] Sadly, that report has itself become a battlefield for controversy, but certain themes are not controversial. Firstly, the report confirms the variety of different decisions, as set out in Table 1. Secondly, Dutch doctors receive considerably more requests for active killing than they accept. Far from relieving the doctor of the necessity, on occasion, to say 'no', the new procedures have increased it. Thirdly, the overwhelming reason that patients give for requesting the procedure is a fear of 'losing control'. Like the process of birth, the process of dying is seen by many as a surrender of control of their lives to others. There is an important message here for all those concerned with the care of the dying. The Working Party documents many cases in which good palliative care has been associated with a patient's sense of a recovery of control. More controversial conclusions from the Dutch report include the fact that doctors do not appear always to adhere to their own guidelines, and the relative lack of hospice care in The Netherlands.[2]

Table 1 Medical Decisions at the End of Life
Active decision to *end* life
—   physician assisted suicide
—   physician assisted death
Active decision *not to prolong* life
—   withholding treatment
—   withdrawing treatment
•   suddenly
•   gradually

During the last twenty-five years there has been a number of significant medical advances affecting medical decisions at the end of life. Perhaps the most significant of these have been in resuscitation, both in respiratory failure and in cardiac arrest. These cases present peculiar, but not novel, problems. When faced with the dilemma of poliomyelitis patients unable to breathe for themselves, but maintained on large, heavy respirators, the Roman Catholic Church distinguished between ordinary and 'extraordinary' methods of keeping people alive. This distinction is equally valid in these more recent problems. In this context 'extraordinary' might be defined as a medical intervention which is burdensome *and* which can serve no plausible therapeutic goal.

It is always easier to elect not to treat a patient than to withdraw treatment once given. Acute emergencies, however, do not give time to weigh up all the issues and the outcome may become apparent only days, or even weeks, later. Doctors then need to review their treatment objectives. Maintenance of the patient's basic functions, with no future prospect of improvement, is difficult to justify, either on medical, philosophical or theological grounds. Since the Working Party reported, the numbers of elderly people have significantly increased and in consequence such dilemmas have become more frequent.

We now have a further twenty-five years' experience of effective palliative care. Many new hospices have opened during this period, often with an overt, but sometimes discreet, religious affiliation and committed to the principles of holistic medicine. There is almost no reason today for patients with an incurable condition to die in agony and distress. Supporters of active killing allege that in fact large numbers of patients still die in such dehumanizing conditions. Indeed they do, and it is a disgrace for the medical profession that it should be so. The comprehensive and universal teaching, together with the investment of resources, which the Working Party envisaged, has simply not happened. Doctors still find death difficult to handle and retreat from it at the slightest opportunity. Ann Cartwright[3] reported more than twenty-five years ago that two-thirds of the district nurses in her survey felt that they would like to be able to give more time to those with terminal illness. That situation has not improved. Indeed, the changes in the National Health Service in recent years have reduced still further the contacts between the dying patient and an experienced, well-trained district nurse. Most patients have noted the progressive loss of tender nursing care from acute hospital wards, as staff numbers have been reduced and the demands upon nursing staff have become technologically more complex.

> A patient was admitted to an acute surgical ward, in the terminal stages of cancer of the prostate. He was confused and disorientated and hardly recognized his family. He seemed in great pain and various suggestions were made for heroic treatment of his urinary symptoms. The relatives obtained a place for him at a local hospice and after major arguments with the surgical team (which would have deterred all but the most determined), succeeded in having him transferred there. One of the surgeons in training even felt it incumbent upon him to telephone the hospice to warn them that the patient was 'unduly sensitive to opioids'.

The hospice ignored this inappropriate and inaccurate advice. Instead, it provided its usual palliative care service, tailored to individual needs. In his remaining four days the patient became more alert, obviously pain- and distress free, and able to converse happily with his relatives. He was even able to make a Christian commitment before dying peacefully surrounded by his family.[4]

This is precisely the initial situation that proponents of active killing might use to justify their cause. It seems to me utterly illogical that, if doctors are guilty of bad terminal care, society should then award them greater powers to remedy the problem. The Working Party itself argued in support of the legal adage that 'bad cases do not make good law'. Surely society should insist that the poor performance of the few, but still too many, doctors is raised to the standards of the average and that the standards of the average should aspire to those of the best?

The outcome of treatment in hospices set out in the above example cannot claim to be without exception. No hospice doctor will provide an absolute guarantee that in all circumstances all pain and distress can be overcome. The Working Party seemed willing to entertain the possibility that in certain rare circumstances active killing might be morally justifiable (see page 10). The examples they give, however, are far removed from the bed of a dying patient. I believe that their doctrine of necessity may occasionally apply in terminal illness. Such a patient would be suffering severe pain which could not be controlled or, perhaps, unrelieved vomiting or severe respiratory distress. These cases are exceptionally rare and would not even be considered until the patient had received treatment from a palliative care specialist and, ideally, the advice of a nationally recognized expert in the field. Most doctors would never see one in a professional lifetime. I have not the slightest doubt that in those most exceptional circumstances, easing the passing of life at the request of the patient would attract the praise, rather than the opprobrium, of the General Medical Council and the courts of law. Society would be singularly misguided, however, to change the legal framework for such exceptional cases. They could easily be contained on an *ad hoc*, individual basis. Changing the law, as the Working Party argued, would be likely to make the exceptional case more common. In the words of a doctor quoted by Professor Richard Hare[5] in 1971, 'we shall start by putting patients away because they are in intolerable pain and haven't long to live anyway; and we shall end up by putting them away because it is Friday afternoon and we want to get away for the weekend'. The House of Lords Select Committee on Medical Ethics, after a most detailed investigation, similarly concluded[6] in 1994, 'there should be no change in the law to permit euthanasia' (para. 237). According to its Chairman, Lord Walton, the Committee was considerably influenced in its unanimous verdict by a visit to Holland. Lord Walton further said, when speaking in the House of Lords about the production of the Select Committee's Report: 'Individual cases cannot reasonably establish a foundation and a policy which would have such serious and widespread repercussions. The issue of euthanasia is one in which the interests of the individual cannot be separated from those of society as a whole.'[7]

The most notable change in disease incidence over the last twenty-five years has been the development of a major epidemic of HIV infection. This has brought the prospect of an early, painful death to an increasing number of (mostly) young men. Yet again the principles advanced by the Working Party are relevant. To impose intrusive resuscitation or excessively demanding treatment on a patient in the terminal stages of AIDS, who does not wish it, is bad medicine, as well as dubious morality. Again, hospices have demonstrated their value in such circumstances and, with the modest success of some expensive treatments, the disease process has at least been slowed, if not yet halted.

Relatives see their loved ones in the final stages of the dying process and inevitably transfer their own emotions of horror and revulsion to the patient. This fuels the demand for active killings. Things are, however, not always what they seem.

> In February 1990 I personally suffered a 'failed' cardiac arrest. The doctors who were expecting my lecture were treated to a horrifying spectacle. My chest was pumped up and down. Electric shocks convulsed my body. Active resuscitation is never a dignified procedure. My own sensations were however totally different. I was overcome by a peace and warmth and comfort, such as I have never known before or since. If this is the process of dying, I look forward to it eagerly.

Euthanasia is one of a number of issues, such as fluoridation, which engage the minds of an articulate minority. They demand advance directives, so that they may control the process of their own dying. It will indeed be most helpful to doctors, in the difficult decisions they face, to know what the patient might have wished in the circumstances. Yet the patient's freedom of choice cannot override that of health care workers, obliging them to act against their own moral principles. Doctors are entitled to relieve an individual's excruciating pain in the interests of patients in adjacent hospital beds whether the individual wishes it or not. Nurses are entitled to keep the patient clean and to offer oral feeding and fluids, even if the patient denies them the right to use artificial forms of nutrition.[8] Parliament is currently considering whether health care professionals should be legally obliged to follow previously expressed 'advance directives'.[9] Any proposed legislation must be sufficiently broadly drawn to ensure that health care workers enjoy a wide discretion in dealing with the practical issues as they arise, which the patient him- or herself may not have foreseen.

Experience suggests that, although it is an articulate minority who would like to see changes in the existing framework, it will be the poor and disadvantaged who suffer from the consequences. It is the most deprived children in our society who pay for the self-determination of the articulate minority opposed to water fluoridation. So it will be with active killing; those who are powerless will be least likely to receive a proper hearing.

Equity demands that the powerless are given the same respect as the powerful. The Church's prophetic witness has always been to the needs of the powerless. It must therefore resist anything that puts them in greater danger.

Some of the most powerless and disadvantaged patients are those severely handicapped and bed-bound following massive strokes. Abandoned by the National Health Service, they are often confined in what have been described as 'warehouses for the elderly'. It is such cases that drive the euthanasia debate in the United States and, increasingly, in this country. Surely, if food and fluids can be withdrawn from patients in the permanent vegetative state[10] they should be withdrawn from patients in deep coma, unable to respond intelligently to the outside world?

> A patient with a massive stroke was admitted to a nursing home and fed by mouth, with difficulty, using protein-concentrated milk. The family insisted that such nutrients should be withdrawn and were most aggressive to nursing staff who offered them surreptitiously. The doctor initially rejected the family's request but later acquiesced. When the patient died, the body weighed 3 stone and 8 lbs (22.7 kg).

A distinction needs to be drawn between intrusive feeding measures and feeding by mouth. In the United States of America, preservation of life seems to be pursued at whatever cost, crippling the family budget. In the United Kingdom, most doctors would not pursue intrusive feeding measures unless they were confident that some real improvement in the patient's condition could reasonably be foreseen. Patients in the persistent vegetative state[11] cannot feel pain although some doctors claim that they may be aware of thirst. To extrapolate from this, fortunately rare, condition to much more common neurological conditions ignores this crucial fact.

If nursing-home patients are literally to be starved to death, it would surely be more humane to kill them with a quick lethal injection. The objection to either course of action is the same. Both are intended to terminate a life that has somehow become inconvenient. At least half of patients with strokes are dead within twelve months. The proportion among massive strokes must be even greater. Is it compassion or patience that is being tested in such cases? It is certainly important for each of us to make our wishes known before such a catastrophe befalls us so that health care professionals may be aware of them during the difficult decisions they will be asked to make. Since less than half the population currently makes a will, however, it seems likely that an even smaller proportion will make a so-called 'living will'. It is difficult to believe that the disadvantaged and the powerless in our society will do so, which is precisely why the doctor must, at all times, act in the patient's best interests. Whilst a member of the family may consider that a given individual would be better off dead than alive, the doctor would be extremely unwise to assume that the patient would take the same view. Moreover there may be many related factors preventing a relative from taking an entirely objective view.

Wilkinson[12] has suggested the basic presuppositions upon which the advocacy of euthanasia is usually based. This essay, like the Working Party's report, has attempted to show that many of these presuppositions are in fact untrue and all of them are open to challenge.

Christians also approach the subject with presuppositions, but they can be confident that even in this postmodern world they remain just as relevant as ever and that they are as sustainable as those of their critics. Indeed, I believe that the more thoroughly the philosophical issues are studied, the greater the validity of the Christian position will be seen to be. I therefore commend this report to you as a highly topical, relevant contribution to the current debate.

Stuart Horner
December 1999

Note: *All text from the first edition has been set in a serif font, and all new material has been set in a sans serif font.*

Preface to the First Edition

Our Working Party was set up in the autumn of 1970 under the auspices of the Church of England's Board for Social Responsibility, and it first met in December of that year under the Chairmanship of the Rt Revd Ian Ramsey, then Bishop of Durham. Its subsequent course has not been smooth. In particular it suffered a grievous loss with the death of its Chairman in October 1972, when, for a time, the continued existence of the group was uncertain. A majority of its members, however, felt that the task should be pursued, and asked the Secretary, Canon Melinsky, to act also as Chairman.

Over the course of three and a half years and 15 meetings there have been some changes in the membership of the group. Originally it comprised in addition to its Chairman: Lord Amulree, the Revd Prof. G. R. Dunstan, Prof. R. M. Hare, Canon M. A. H. Melinsky (Secretary), Prof. B. G. Mitchell, Chancellor the Revd E. Garth Moore, The Bishop of Exeter (The Rt Revd R. C. Mortimer), and Dr Cicely Saunders. In January 1971 Miss V. Pritchard joined the group to represent the nursing profession, but a change of appointment compelled her resignation in January 1974. The Bishop of Exeter withdrew in July 1971, but continued for a time to receive the group's working papers. At the end of 1972 the group accepted with regret the resignation of Professor Dunstan, and welcomed in his place Professor Baelz. Latterly, Lord Amulree has not been able to attend meetings, but has been kind enough to maintain an advisory brief in matters medical.

The group has done its utmost to listen to and understand the case put forward by advocates of voluntary euthanasia, and it has given much time and care to examining in detail case histories of patients with terminal illnesses. It has also visited a hospice devoted to the care of such patients, and members talked with some of them and with the staff who care for them. It has received much written evidence, and is glad to record its indebtedness to the following for their spoken evidence:

> Dr Hugh Faulkner, general practitioner, and Medical Secretary of the Medical Practitioners' Union.

> Professor John Hinton, Professor of Psychiatry, Middlesex Hospital Medical School, London.

> Sir John Stallworthy, former Nuffield Professor of Obstetrics and Gynaecology, University of Oxford.

Dr Bleddyn Davies, Department of Social Science and Administration, the London School of Economics and Political Science.

Dr Maurice Millard, former general practitioner, and member of the Voluntary Euthanasia Society.

Dr John Agate, Consultant in Geriatrics, Ipswich and East Suffolk Hospitals.

As the investigation proceeded the complexity of the issues involved became more apparent, and it was decided that members should contribute to the final report from their own particular disciplines and areas of experience, even at the cost of a certain loss of homogeneity. Readers skilled in source-criticism may detect behind Chapter 1 the hand of Prof. Mitchell; behind Chapter 2 the hands of Prof. Mitchell and Prof. Hare; behind Chapter 3 the hands of Prof. Baelz and Prof. Hare; behind Chapters 4 and 5 the hand of Dr Saunders; and behind Chapter 6 the hand of Chancellor Garth Moore.[1] Prof. Mitchell and the Chairman have acted as general editors to give the final report as much consistency in argument and style as possible. The Conclusions that form Chapter 7 are unanimously agreed by all the members of the group, although they wish to state that not every member would be prepared to subscribe absolutely to every statement in the report.

The Working Party records its gratitude to the Editor and publishers of *Theology* for allowing it to make use in Chapter 3 of part of an article by Prof. Baelz which first appeared in that journal in May 1972. It is also happy to express its appreciation to Miss Lydia Hodges and Miss Tessa Perfect for their care and diligence in the typing and retyping of successive drafts.

It now presents this report in the hope that it may be widely read and considered as a responsible Anglican contribution to a continuing debate which has serious implications not only for the welfare of many individuals but also for the well-being of society.

M. A. H. Melinsky (Chairman)
Amulree
P. R. Baelz
R. M. Hare
B. G. Mitchell
E. Garth Moore
C. Saunders

1 October 1974

1

Introduction

No discussion of voluntary euthanasia would, or should, carry conviction, if it failed to take seriously the human realities of senility and death. Accordingly we start with individual cases and return to them and others like them later in our report. Here are four sent to us by the Voluntary Euthanasia Society.

Case History A (submitted by a general practitioner)

Miss B., aged 75, before she herself was stricken, had over the years discussed voluntary euthanasia with me. She made it very clear that she agreed entirely with the 'Right to Die with Dignity', and that she would expect me to do my part to ensure this, should the occasion arise. Unhappily, in due course, she developed suspicious abdominal symptoms, was admitted to hospital, operated on, and found to have cancer of the head of the pancreas, with secondary deposits already present in the liver and lymph glands.

She had palliative surgery and was sent home with a hopeless prognosis – probably three to four months to live at the outside.

She had little pain, but developed jaundice and ascites (fluid in the abdomen), which made her very distended, and could only be relieved by repeated paracentesis (tapping of the fluid). By this time my patient, who had become very weak and emaciated owing to constant vomiting which it was difficult to allay, began daily to remind me of our previous conversations, and I replied that I was seeing her twice a day and would always do my best for her. While I pondered what the 'best' should be, her brother-in-law (who was a minister of religion) and sister (a lawyer) requested my presence at a bedside farewell service. When I arrived she was too weak to speak, but whispered 'Tonight, please', and her eyes met mine.

1

A prayer was said, a hymn was sung, and she died peacefully that night after receiving a quite modest dose of morphine. It was my clear moral duty not to allow her to regain consciousness and I returned to make sure that she was at peace later.

Case History B (submitted by a general practitioner)

A sad case which hangs rather heavily on my conscience was that of an old lady of 90 who for many years suffered from rheumatic arthritis. Finally she became totally disabled and blind and spent the last year or two of her life in a nursing home. She was never really free from pain in spite of analgesics, and from about the age of 85 became very depressed and tired of living. A consultant psychiatrist prescribed antidepressant drugs for her, but, predictably, these had little effect, as her depression was reactive to her handicapped existence. She repeatedly asked for euthanasia but I stalled her off, as her heart was sound, she ate well, and her mind was clear. Finally, she mercifully developed pneumonia, antibiotics were withheld, and she died peacefully. If euthanasia had been legalized, she would have been spared at least one year of unhappy existence, and it was interesting that, when she finally died, the Matron of the Home, who was a Roman Catholic, concurred with my views and would perhaps have acquiesced in any merciful step I might have taken months previously. This type of case is liable to disturb one's conscience for not doing quite enough for aged suffering humanity.

Case History C (from a letter published by the Voluntary Euthanasia Society)

My husband died from leukaemia three years ago at the age of 79. When I realized he could never recover but was only being kept 'alive' by constant drugs which were having *disastrous* effects, I explained to the doctor (and specialist) how I felt . . . but to no avail, and for twelve months he was allowed to continue in a state of both physical and mental agony. I could only feel *relief* at his ultimate release. We had enjoyed fifty years of wonderful companionship (I am 81 and a half). The strain of those agonizing months (and the suppressed *rebellion* at such treatment, insisted on to no purpose) resulted in my having a stroke three months later. Mercifully this has affected me only physically – and so far my brain is virile and active (*too* active in fact!).

Case History D (from a letter published by the Voluntary Euthanasia Society)

I have no family commitments. I suffer from diabetes, failing eyesight, skin disorders, arthritis and chronic narrowing of the arteries which has already resulted in the amputation of a leg . . . Once I become a burden to society I shall want to opt out. I am not afraid of death, but I am afraid of the protracted suffering which would almost certainly precede my death in the natural course of events. Even more, I am afraid of the consequences of making an unsuccessful suicide attempt. During the six months I spent in hospital last year, numerous were the patients brought in for resuscitation after suicide attempts, and the memory of the sordid and horrifying sounds which ensued from behind the screens will never leave me. When the time comes, I shall need help, and it would be a great comfort to me to know that there is a doctor to whom I can turn.

It is impossible to read these stories without asking the question whether everything was done that could and should have been done to care for and comfort these men and women in their severe distress. We must overcome our contemporary reluctance to talk of death and dying and face the problem that these unhappy cases represent. Men should be enabled to 'die well'. This is the literal meaning of the word 'euthanasia' and, if we were starting afresh, there would be a good case for using this word to express our common concern for the welfare of the dying. But this is no longer practicable, since the word has now become established in popular usage with a more precise meaning. In this sense to administer euthanasia means the deliberate ending of life because this is believed to be, in the circumstances, the only way of enabling the patient to die in dignity and peace.

The question whether euthanasia, in this sense, should be permitted by law raises moral problems of fundamental importance and considerable difficulty, and it is inevitable that a great part of our report should be addressed to it. Parliament has on two occasions in this century had before it proposals for legislation and may have again. But it would be a very great mistake for those who are deeply concerned about the welfare of the dying to think that they had discharged their duty when they had reached a conclusion on this question. And so we shall try to keep the larger problem of the care of the dying before our minds. While, therefore, in what follows, we shall assess carefully, and at times criticize stringently, the case for voluntary euthanasia, we recognize and share the profound concern of its proponents that men should be enabled to die well; and among them we acknowledge the work of the Voluntary Euthanasia Society in helping to direct public attention to the way in which social changes and medical advances have tended in some respects to make this more difficult than it used to be.

Since the euthanasia debate has centred on possible legislation, we shall begin by examining the actual Bills presented to Parliament in 1936 and 1969 and the arguments by which they were supported. We shall then, in Chapters 2 and 3, discuss the moral and theological issues involved in their own right. In Chapter 4 we come back to the cases we started with and others like them, before in Chapter 5 turning to the larger question of the positive steps that need to be taken in the care of the dying and chronically sick. In Chapter 6 we examine the present law of homicide and consider some of the implications of legalizing voluntary euthanasia. In this way we hope to do justice to the case for voluntary euthanasia and to make a serious contribution to solving the problem which it seeks to remedy.

2

Moral Considerations

There have been two Voluntary Euthanasia Bills presented to Parliament, one in 1936, the other in 1969.[1] It is appropriate to consider and compare these Bills and to ask what is the moral position which underlies each of them. When this is done it becomes apparent that they differ significantly in scope and emphasis.

(i) In the Voluntary Euthanasia Bill of 1936 euthanasia was to be restricted to patients suffering from a disease which was 'incurable, fatal and painful'. It was for the patient to request euthanasia, but there was no question of his being able to demand it as a right. Hence the problem was discussed primarily as one of medical ethics.[2] It may in certain circumstances be necessary to choose between the preservation of life and the relief of suffering, and in such a case it is argued that compassion demands the relief of suffering. The supporters of the legislation argued that the medical prolongation of life made possible by technical advances had increased the proportion of cases in which this dilemma was posed. But the cases they specified were those in which the disease was both incurable and fatal and it was generally assumed in the discussion that euthanasia should be contemplated only in the terminal stage of such an illness. Hence in the debate in the House of Lords[3] a good deal of attention was paid to the question whether doctors who at present prescribe increased doses of pain-killing drugs, at the risk of shortening life, are in effect conceding the principle of euthanasia. The situation envisaged as that which alone might justify euthanasia was one in which the doctor who had embarked upon this policy found that he could no longer control the pain and was therefore faced with the choice of ending the patient's life or failing to control the pain.

(ii) The Voluntary Euthanasia Bill of 1969 provided that the patient or prospective patient should be able to sign in advance a declaration requesting the administration of euthanasia to himself if he was believed to be suffering from 'a serious physical illness or impairment reasonably thought in the patient's case to be incurable and expected to cause him severe distress or render him incapable of rational existence'. The circumstances regarded as justifying euthanasia differed in two important respects from those envisaged in the earlier Bill:

(a)   The requirement that the condition be fatal was omitted; it sufficed that it be incurable.

(b)   'Incapacity for rational existence' was added to 'expected to cause severe distress'.

These alterations involve a considerable extension of the range of cases to which euthanasia would become applicable. They would cover, and were intended to cover, chronic conditions that are distressing but not fatal, and also senile dementia. The extension follows naturally from the sort of justification afforded. The individual is conceived to enjoy, in some sense, a right to die; it is for him, therefore, other things being equal, to specify the conditions under which that right is to be exercised. Although the doctor must take a decision, and may on conscientious grounds decline to act, he exercises his professional judgement as a doctor only to the extent of certifying that the circumstances are those that the law specifies as justifying euthanasia. There is, once this type of justification is urged, a shift in the onus of proof. It would be for society to show reason why limits should be imposed in the interests of others upon the individual's *prima facie* right to have his life terminated when, in his own judgement, it is not worth living. The question then arises: given a 'right to die', what reason could society show why that right should be circumscribed to the extent laid down in the Bill? Why, for example, should the right to euthanasia be restricted to severe physical illness? Is not mental illness, even when – perhaps especially when – it falls short of total incapacity for rational existence, as distressing as physical illness? And who, in any case, is to judge how severe is the distress and whether it is severe enough to warrant euthanasia? On the principles underlying the Bill it would seem appropriate that the decision should rest with the individual whose right to die is being invoked. It is true that society as a whole has an interest in the preservation of life, and that this interest needs to be protected, but once the individual's right to die has been conceded, it is not enough to appeal to some such general consideration. It becomes necessary to show that society has an overriding interest in the preservation of *this individual's* life, for, unless this can be shown, he must be presumed free to exercise his right to die. If, for example, he has dependents who need him or who would miss him, or if he has a positive contribution of a recognizable kind which he could still make to the well-being of others, these could be sufficient grounds for denying him, in the general interest, the exercise of his right to die. Otherwise, society would not be morally entitled to interfere. Hence it would be necessary to attempt to estimate the value of the individual's life to the community, and, even if this were thought morally acceptable, it would raise serious practical problems. It is likely that few advocates of 'the right to die' have in fact wished to license any such developments. The point is, simply, that this is the logic of their position if the right to die is taken to imply, as is normal with rights, a correlative duty on the part of others to secure to the individual the exercise of his right. Such a duty would also conflict with, and possibly erode, the general assumption that life ought to be protected.

One influence contributing to the concept of a right to die has undoubtedly been a particular interpretation of the Suicide Act of 1961, which some take to imply that suicide is morally permissible and to have created a legal right to die. Thus it has been argued that, as it is not a criminal offence to commit or attempt to commit suicide, the law concedes the right of the individual to end his own life. It is, indeed, sometimes suggested that the right to die has the same moral status, and has now been given the same legal status, as the right to live. It is claimed in effect that the individual has a right to self-determination in the matter of life and death – that, if he chooses to live, there is a duty upon others to protect his life, and that, equally, if he chooses to die, there is a duty upon others to assist his dying. The position is, admittedly, somewhat unclear, but the probability is that the Suicide Act recognizes no such moral right and confers no such legal right. The individual is free to take his own life; he has a 'mere liberty' to do so, that is to say, it is not a criminal offence, but Parliament has made it a criminal offence to aid or abet his suicide. It is probably not a criminal offence to resuscitate a person who has attempted suicide; and it is, at the least, extremely doubtful whether he could succeed in an action at civil law against anyone who resuscitated him. Hence, if voluntary euthanasia were to be legalized, it would involve a new departure from the principles underlying the present law.

It is safe to assume, however, that many of those who have used the expression 'a right to die' have not intended it to be taken in the strong sense that we have been considering. It may often amount to no more than a plea to be allowed to die in peace and dignity without the application of useless remedies. Many of the cases to which the Voluntary Euthanasia Society calls attention are cases where the patient has been subjected to medical treatment of a troublesome kind in order to secure a minimal extension of life when what he needs is the sort of care that will help him to die in peace.[4] We agree with the Society that there comes a point in the course of a fatal illness when the doctor's duty to the patient is no longer to use all efforts to preserve his life, but rather to care for him and comfort him in his dying.[5] The Society would, however, go further than this and argue that there are circumstances in which this very duty of caring for the dying entails a duty actually to end the patient's life. It is this alleged duty on the part of the doctor which they sometimes have in mind when they talk of the patient's 'right to die'. This brings us back to the first approach to voluntary euthanasia, which we took to characterize the Voluntary Euthanasia Bill of 1936.

Before turning to that Bill we wish to express our strong dissent from the use of the expression 'right to die' in the discussion of euthanasia. It suffers from a dangerous ambiguity, as we have seen, and serves to mask three quite distinct demands:

(i)   that the individual should in principle be free to determine whether he shall live or die and that, in the event of his choosing to die, he should be entitled to be assisted in so doing by the medical profession, except in so far as his rights are limited in the general interest;

(ii)   that a doctor should with the patient's consent be free, under certain safeguards, to end the patient's life in cases (if there are such) where it is medically impossible to control the pain;

(iii)   that

      (a) a patient *in extremis* should not be subjected to troublesome treatments which cannot restore him to health, and

      (b) doctors may use drugs to control pain even at the risk of shortening life.

Demand (iii) does not involve euthanasia at all, for it does not involve deliberately killing the patient. (i) involves euthanasia on a different basis from (ii) and on a larger scale. An expression which suffers from this degree of ambiguity is dangerously unsuitable for use in serious discussion.

That (iii) does not involve euthanasia at all is not always recognized. With respect to (iii) (a) there is a tendency in the literature of the Voluntary Euthanasia Society to protest, with entire justification, against 'keeping people alive' against their will, and to assume that anyone who endorses this protest has automatically accepted the principle that, in the sort of circumstances envisaged, life may deliberately be ended. With respect to (iii) (b) Professor Joseph Fletcher has given currency to the term 'indirect euthanasia' as applied to cases of this sort, and, as we have seen, it was claimed in the House of Lords Debate on the 1936 Bill that doctors already accepted the principle of euthanasia in so far as they were prepared to use pain-killing drugs in this way. Thus it is argued that: 'It is true, generally speaking, that "a good doctor does not let his patient die in pain" because in the last phase of life most doctors today will not hesitate to give him whatever narcotics and/or sedatives may be necessary to dull his perception of pain or reduce him to a semi-conscious condition. If that policy shortens the patient's life, even by a few hours, the doctor is, in fact, practising euthanasia, although not strictly *voluntary* euthanasia.'[6]

There is in all medical treatment a degree of risk to the patient which has to be assessed in relation to the good which it is hoped to achieve. When the patient is in the terminal stage of a fatal illness and there is no longer any hope of a cure or of a worthwhile alleviation of the disease, the good to be achieved is his comfort and peace of mind. The appropriate treatment is therefore good nursing care and the use of pain-killing drugs where necessary. It is wrong to think that medicine has now no more to do; it has a function that requires skill, care and attention of a high order.[7] In this situation a greater risk of shortening life is acceptable than when other treatments are in question. But for the doctor to take measures deliberately to kill the patient (whether or not he would be *justified* in doing so) involves a definite, and in its implications momentous, change of policy. There is a clear distinction to be drawn between rendering someone unconscious at the risk of killing him and killing him in order to render him unconscious. In the kind of situation we are envisaging it is easy for those who do not have to make the decisions to regard such discrimination as unnecessarily fine, but its importance tends to be intuitively evident to those upon whom the burden of decision rests. There is a decisive difference between the situation of a medical practitioner whose patient dies as the result of an increased dosage of a pain-killing drug and who would have used a safer drug had it been available, and that of a public executioner, in states which employ this means of carrying out the death penalty, who chooses his drug for its death-inducing properties. Two rivers may take their rise at a very little distance from one another on a mountainous plateau, but this slight difference may determine that the one flows north and the other south.

There is nothing, therefore, in the law as it stands or in currently accepted medical practice which implies that it is either legally or morally permissible to kill the patient with or without his consent. And much, though not all, of the case for voluntary euthanasia would be met by wider recognition of the limits to be set upon attempts to prolong life when further treatment offers no reasonable hope of recovery or significant alleviation. However, when all the ambiguities have been removed, there remains for consideration the claim that there are circumstances in which the doctor's duty to the patient can be discharged only by a deliberate decision to end his life; and that, if this is so, the law ought to be altered so as to give the practice explicit recognition. It will be apparent that there are a number of different points at which this claim might be called in question. It might be denied that there could even in principle ever be cases in which such action was justified. It might be conceded that such cases are conceivable, but maintained that in actual medical practice they do not or need not occur. It might be agreed that there are such cases, but argued nevertheless that a professional ethic which tried to take account of them would run too grave a risk of failing to ensure the right decision on most occasions. If this risk were thought to be acceptable, and the profession were satisfied that the exceptional cases could be adquately specified, it is arguable that the dangers that might be expected to attend any alteration in the law are so considerable that it would be better to allow hard cases to be taken care of by the various expedients that are at present available.

The problem is thus a complex one and it is as well to recognize this from the start. Even if the solution should be found to lie in the acceptance of a simple principle, it is not a simple matter to show that this is so. The principle that it is wrong to take innocent life is one that everyone may be presumed to accept; the question is whether there can ever be exceptions to it and precisely what would be involved in the admission of exceptions. There are extreme situations, outside the medical field, in which men have killed others to avoid their suffering severely and pointlessly. We have spent much time considering cases, such as are occasionally reported in the newspapers, of drivers who have been trapped in vehicles which have caught fire after accidents and who have begged the bystanders to kill them as painlessly as possible so that they will not burn to death as is otherwise inevitable. In war similar cases occur of men trapped in blazing gun-turrets, and of wounded who face death by torture if left on the battlefield.

We have not found it possible to say that in these desperate situations those who killed acted wrongly, and to this extent, at least, it has to be accepted that the prohibition against killing the innocent does not hold entirely without exception. Yet to declare that 'it is not always wrong to kill the innocent; it is only generally wrong' would be to deprive the principle of the sanctity which we feel it to possess. It is the same with other moral principles that we hold with the utmost seriousness: that it is wrong to torture, to falsify evidence, to discriminate on grounds of race. It is hard to be sure that there may not occur extreme situations in which to breach them would be the lesser evil. In such circumstances the severity of the dilemma is in proportion to the sacredness of the principle which a person is forced to violate.

Presumably the reason for our reluctance to say in such cases 'it is not always wrong' is not simply that we fear the consequences in practice of admitting exceptions to the principle, but also that when we normally distinguish between 'what is always wrong' and 'what is generally wrong', we do so against a background of assumptions, one of which is that we are operating within the conditions of life that we normally encounter. Our fear is that, if the principle is once so qualified as to allow for the altogether exceptional cases, it will be regarded as no longer binding in the ordinary conduct of life.

However, even if it is conceded that there may be extreme cases in which the taking of innocent life is justified in order to prevent intolerable and uncontrollable suffering, it remains to ask whether such cases occur in medical practice and whether the ethic of the medical profession can properly regard them as exceptions to the principle of not taking innocent life. There is then the further question whether the law should be altered so as to take account of them.

The medical issue is discussed elsewhere in this report.[8] The cases in question are those, if any there are, in which the pain is such that it does not yield to medical treatment of any kind (or to the medical treatment that is, or could be made, available), and in which the patient is in the terminal stage of a fatal illness. These would resemble the extreme situations already mentioned in that the killing would be undertaken as being the only way of saving the individual from a death that is in any case imminent and is reasonably expected to be intolerably painful. We have to ask whether it is possible to specify these cases precisely enough in advance to prevent the class of exceptional cases being continuously expanded under the pressure of the many motives, both good and bad, that are bound to be operative. The difficulty of so doing is evidenced by the course of the entire euthanasia debate. There is, as we have already seen, considerable divergence of opinion among supporters of voluntary euthanasia as to the range and type of cases to be covered, and we may be sure that, however restrictive the formula adopted, it would inevitably be open to very wide differences of interpretation. It is for reasons of this sort that a professional ethic cannot be built on altogether exceptional circumstances, even if in some such exceptional cases a man who contravened it might rightly be held not to be morally culpable. Thus, no matter how extreme the emergency, the code of the policeman cannot countenance torture or the falsification of evidence.

If this is true of the accepted ethics of the medical profession, it is even more obviously true of the law. It is perfectly consistent to argue that morally speaking euthanasia is permissible in some extreme cases, but that it would be wrong to alter the law to allow it in such cases, because this might inescapably, in practice, let in cases in which euthanasia should not be allowed by law. The law is a blunt instrument for dealing with moral complexities and it is better to allow hard cases to be taken care of by the various expedients that are available than to introduce a new principle which would turn out to be too permissive.

This could happen in practice because of the difficulty, amounting to an impossibility, of finding a form of words which cannot with plausibility be interpreted more widely than was originally intended – and it is relevant that courts of law in interpreting statutes are not bound by the intentions of the legislator. This may be illustrated from the text of the 1969 Voluntary Euthanasia Bill. It would have to be certified that the patient was believed to be suffering from 'a serious physical illness or impairment reasonably thought in the patient's case to be incurable and expected to cause him severe distress or to render him incapable of rational existence'. The expression 'physical illness' is presumably intended to rule out mental illness as a ground for euthanasia, but it could plausibly be argued, and almost certainly would be argued, that most, if not all, mental illnesses have a physical basis. It is very difficult to believe that the restriction to 'physical illness' as commonly understood could be made effective, and this would result not from any failure in rationality, or good faith, but from the inherent difficulty of drawing a clear line in such a case. The same problem might be expected to arise in connection with 'severe' distress and 'incapable of rational existence'. These are matters of degree, and whereas there are extreme cases in which there can be no doubt as to the applicability of such terms there is no clear line of demarcation between these and more disputable ones. We have already seen that the support for voluntary euthanasia comes from a variety of bodies of opinion with differing views as to the range of cases that it should cover. Those who favour the widest possible extension would quite properly endeavour to secure the most liberal possible interpretation of the law, as has happened in the case of the Abortion Act 1967; and the resulting pressure, because of the inevitable imprecision of the key expressions, would be extremely hard to resist.

The conclusion that euthanasia ought not to be legalized is, therefore, forced upon us independently of any consideration of the practical difficulties and social effects that might be expected to attend a change in the law. But these are in themselves enough to awaken serious doubts even in those who might otherwise be inclined to support the proposal. It is essential that any legalized form of euthanasia should be voluntary and no responsible body has yet suggested otherwise. Since the patient who is a candidate for euthanasia is *ex hypothesi* not in a condition to make a rational choice at the time when it would need to be administered, consent can be secured only by a previous declaration. The declaration has to be formally registered if abuse is to be prevented. Something like the arrangements proposed in the 1969 Bill would seem to be essential. But these arrangements presuppose a reasonable man who decides upon due deliberation that he wishes euthanasia to be administered to him in certain circumstances and remains thereafter capable of deciding with equal rationality whether he shall adhere to his resolution or cancel it. He must be in his right mind when he signs the declaration (need he be when he wants to cancel it?). In any case it will fall to someone to decide whether he is in his right mind or not, and problems are likely to arise at that point. While there are, no doubt, among intellectuals in particular, persons who can make and adhere to a rational decision of this kind in the circumstances of severe illness, they are not likely to be numerous. Many more would fluctuate according to their mood and, as their condition deteriorated, it would become increasingly hazardous to determine whether they still understood what they had decided earlier and wished to abide by it. On those who had as yet made no declaration the pressures would be considerable. They could scarcely remain unaware of the possibility (would it be someone's duty, even, to bring it to their attention?). A decision would be required of them where now there is no possibility of decision. In place of a presumption that those who are ill and all who have to do with them should hope for recovery, so long as that is possible, and prepare for death with patient acceptance when that is inevitable, there would, in every case, be another option which, whatever the attitudes adopted to it, would invite dissension and uncertainty. The attitudes might be very various. There might be some families which were united in favour of euthansia and whose members were composed enough to let the arrangements for it go forward without undue tension or distress. But it is hard to believe that there would not be many more who would experience doubt, hesitation, suspicion and guilt at a time when they would desire to be of one mind. The old would be compelled to raise with themselves the question whether they should prolong the burden upon their families and others who cared for them, and it would require more than ordinary serenity and faith not to wonder whether there were some who wanted them out of the way. It is sometimes said[9] that the wish not to be a burden in such circumstances would be a credit to the sick person, and could in any case be granted only if two doctors (one of consultant status) acceded to it. But this rejoinder misses the point. Our concern is not for the minority who know what they are about and whose families share their determination, but for the far larger number who, vulnerable to social pressures which they do not fully comprehend, may be frightened or confused.

It would be possible to develop in greater detail the deleterious consequences that might be expected to flow from the legalizing of euthanasia. Experience of the Abortion Act 1967, for example, suggests that deliberate abuse of the provisions cannot be ruled out. But to do so might have the effect of obscuring the main argument, and to some extent of falsifying it, by suggesting that we can predict with reasonable certainty what the social effects of the proposed legislation would be, whereas the only thing we can be reasonably sure about is that they would be in large measure unpredicted and enormously difficult to control. In matters so fundamental to our well-being as those of life and death we interfere at our peril with deeply felt attitudes and convictions.

3

Theological Considerations

In the preceding chapter we considered the legislation that has been proposed and the arguments by which it has been supported, and in so doing expressed certain judgements on the moral issues involved. In the present chapter we wish to discuss these issues in the light of theological considerations.

Moral debate is carried on in the language of rights, principles and interests. When Christians join in the discussion they will often use the same language and put forward the same kinds of argument as those who do not share their Christian faith. This makes discussion possible. Were there no agreement whatsoever either in the form or in the substance of the discussion, there would be no dialogue, only confrontation. Nevertheless, differences exist. Presuppositions and approach are not the same. For the Christian, we must not forget, moral debate takes place within a context of religious belief and aspiration. Fundamental to his point of view is the conviction that the overarching reality of human life, indeed of all life, is God. God is the One who creates, redeems and brings to perfection. From him, in him and towards him men live and move and have their being. Not only are they his creatures, they are also called to be his sons, to respond faithfully and joyfully to the claims of his love as embodied and expressed in Jesus Christ. For the Christian, therefore, moral reflection and decision are embedded in his total relationship to God, and moral language is delicately interwoven with religious language. Freedom is set within a context of obedience, responsibility within a context of divine invitation and grace.

The links between religious beliefs and moral principles may be understood in a variety of ways. Some will hold that a body of moral teaching may be derived from the scriptures or from Natural Law. The scriptures, it is said, contain 'the "Maker's instructions" as to how the creatures he has made can best live lives which are satisfying to themselves and beneficial to others'.[1] Natural Law is that aspect of divine eternal law which concerns human beings and which is capable of rational discovery. Even on these views such moral teaching has to be interpreted and clarified, and then applied to new problems and new situations as they arise. Others will be less sanguine about the value of these approaches. It is not so much that they question the authority of the scriptures or the appeal to rational reflection on what makes human life human. It is rather that they sense the variety of conclusions which may be drawn from such data and are conscious of the fact that new situations may render old moral rules obsolete. Consequently they are inclined to speak of the aims and directions of human life which Christian belief implies and to contrast general principles with specific rules. Thus the links between belief and prescription will be loose and informal. But that is not to deny that they in fact exist. For example, the Christian sees man's life both as gift and as calling. He holds it in trust from God to whom he is ultimately responsible. Response to the demanding love of God in all things and through all things is to be the fundamental motive and goal of action.

It follows that the actual claims of other human beings are not the only claims that the Christian has to consider. Even were their interests in no way impaired by what he had in mind to do, he would still feel that he was not absolutely free to do whatever he wished. Consequently he can claim no inalienable right to death on the grounds that his life is his own, and that after due consideration has been given to the interests of other men and women, he may do with it exactly as he pleases. No doubt it is in general a good and valid principle that, so far as possible, men should be allowed to do what they choose. In certain situations emphatic affirmation of this principle may be the only way to establish the importance of individual liberty and responsibility. But freedom to choose is not the whole story about man. He has a divinely offered future and destiny. He is made in the image of God and for the worship and enjoyment of God. He is free, but he also belongs. He belongs to God, 'in whose service is perfect freedom'.

Christians and others will for the most part agree on what constitutes man's interests. However, because Christians believe what others do not believe, namely, that man has a future and a destiny in and for God, agreement will not be total. Nor will it do justice to the Christian point of view to say simply that it ascribes to man certain *additional* interests. Such 'additional' interests may subtly but decisively shape and colour his other interests. Thus Christian moral judgements may, though they will not necessarily, diverge from those of others in cases in which what seems to be at stake is the assessment of man's 'ordinary' interests.

More common today than an immediate appeal to Natural Law or to the scriptures is an appeal through and beyond both to the doctrine of God as Creator. The doctrine in itself does not seem to carry with it any specific moral commands or prohibitions. No immediate deductions concerning the moral life can be compellingly made. But it is said that since God is our Creator, it is not for us to determine the bounds of our mortal life. 'The Lord gave and the Lord hath taken away: blessed be the name of the Lord.'[2] Here we must tread cautiously. Certainly Christians will want to say that human life, as indeed the whole created order, is a gift from God and ultimately depends on him. On the other hand they will equally want to say that men are called to exercise their freedom responsibly under God and to be his 'fellow-workers'. The problem concerns the bounds which their obedience to God and dependence on him place upon the exercise of their freedom. These bounds have been drawn differently in different ages. Take the parallel doctrine of God as Provider. It was once assumed that God set each of us in his appointed social station, and that this set limits to the sphere in which he might exercise his responsible Christian liberty. Few would espouse such a view today. Furthermore, most Christians would agree that it is right to have some say in the question when another life should begin. They accept the claims of responsible parenthood, even if they may differ concerning the ways in which such responsibility is to be exercised. Nor is there any objection to attempts to prolong life beyond the span of threescore years and ten, or even fourscore years, provided that the means for so doing are reasonable and appropriate. Nor again do we believe, as we have already stressed, that there is any objection to the view that 'a patient *in extremis* should not be subjected to troublesome treatments which cannot restore him to health, and that doctors may use drugs to control pain even at the risk of shortening life'.[3] That God is our Creator, that there is a dimension of sheer givenness to all creaturely existence, that we owe him the allegiance of heart and mind – these are all important and basic Christian beliefs; but they do not tell us forthwith in what ways it is fitting that we should express our allegiance, nor do they mark out what is right and what is wrong in each specific situation. Further principles are necessary. It is the task of moral theology to set forth these principles and to suggest their application.

One possible way of developing moral reflection on the basis of a doctrine of Creation might be as follows. Respect for God's creation requires us to refrain from any unnecessary destruction of it. Some measure of destruction, however, is inevitable and necessary. In an ideal world this might not be the case, but in the world in which we find ourselves life can be sustained only at the expense of other life. Such necessity, however, does not justify any wholesale or indiscriminate destruction. When men are faced with the choice of destroying or not destroying, the burden of proof rests with those who wish to destroy. Destruction will be morally justifiable only if the good sought outweighs the evil done and only if that good cannot be secured in any other less destructive way. Now man is the highest order of life on this earth. In religious language, he is made in the image of God. In non-religious language, he is a rational being, a person, whose potentiality for widely ranging experiences and for deeply felt relationships gives him more intrinsic value than that belonging to any other creature. It is generally thought morally justifiable for him to take the life of other animals if this is necessary to provide him with adequate food, but it will seldom be morally justifiable to take a human life, whether his own or that of another. The idea of the sanctity of human life expresses this deep-seated principle. Nevertheless, the prohibition against taking human life is not absolute. There may in certain cases be moral justification for such destruction. For example, it would generally be held to be morally justifiable to shoot one man in order to prevent his throwing a bomb at a crowd. Or, again, in the case considered earlier,[4] few would think a person morally blameworthy if he shot a comrade trapped in a gun-turret in order to put him out of his misery. Even so, although he had in this instance done the only right and possible thing, the person concerned might continue to feel a deep horror at what he had had to do, precisely because he held strongly to the general principle that it is wrong to take innocent life. It would seem, therefore, that where there are other means available of exercising care and compassion towards a person in his dying and of relieving his ultimate distress, respect for God's creation and for the consequent value of human life in general would tell against the practice of euthanasia, or direct killing.

Some may think that the force of this argument – and it could be developed in more detail and with greater precision – is, granted the basic doctrine of Creation, persuasive. Others, however, may feel that the doctrine of Creation so expressed is too static. In asserting that all life *has been* created by God, and that there should be no destructive interference with creation unless it is inevitable, it leaves out of account, it may be said, the ongoing creative activity of God and the high calling of man to share in that activity. The creation of new value is as important as, if not more important than, the preservation of existing value. And it could be argued, paradoxically but not nonsensically, that greater value could be achieved in a person's life, *taken as a whole*, if he knew that at a certain stage of his dying he would be painlessly put to death rather than be allowed to linger on, feeling himself a burden to others as well as to himself. In certain circumstances his death could be said to be a good rather than an evil. The act of physical destruction, it could then be argued, would be a morally creative act. Such, presumably, would be the view of those Christians who hold that voluntary euthanasia is, in certain circumstances, not incompatible with their belief in and allegiance to God.

To explore this issue further we have to ask how death itself is to be characterized within a horizon of Christian meaning. It is not simply a natural occurrence, although it is certainly that. By some their death is naturally welcomed, and in terms of nature it may even be said that death serves life and to that extent is good, for in dying room is made for other living things. But in death as in life a Christian has to do with God. Death has a godward dimension as well as manward and natural dimensions. How, then, is a Christian to understand it?

One line of thought has proceeded on the assumption that death, at least man's death, is the divinely appointed consequence of sin. It is possible to argue on that basis that it is not for the sinner to anticipate that judgement and make himself or another his own executioner, thus 'cheating justice'. An argument like this, however, depends for its validity on a highly dubious concept of the justice of God, and we need not consider it any further.

Nevertheless, it may still represent a valid insight to describe death as man's 'last enemy'. Thus 'the Christian . . . accepts death as that signal occasion when he is finally to prove the love and power of God in Christ. He sees death as the last and crucial occasion for the testing of his faith, where victory is to be won in Christ and his redemption is fulfilled.'[5] Thus the doctrine of Redemption as well as the doctrine of Creation must be allowed to illuminate the issues surrounding man's death. Because death is the destruction of man himself and of all his powers, the faith which conquers death must be a faith which throws itself entirely on the being and love of God, a faith which finds a meaning in death, not in anything which man himself can achieve, nor indeed in the nothingness of final extinction, but only in what God can and will achieve. Adherence to God is through acceptance and passivity. 'At that moment when I feel I am losing hold of myself and am absolutely passive within the hands of the great unknown forces that have formed me . . . O God, grant that I may understand that it is You (provided only my faith is strong enough) who are painfully parting the fibres of my being in order to penetrate to the very marrow of my substance and bear me away within Yourself.'[6]

For the Christian, then, death signifies the ultimate helplessness of man before God and his ultimate dependence on God. His faith bids him wait upon God in patience and in hope. It is this insight, it seems, which prompts the almost universal Christian feeling that suicide is wrong. Perhaps, too, it accounts for the revealing confession of W. R. Inge, who ended his arguments in favour of modifying the traditional Christian view of suicide with the remark: 'At the same time I hope, inconsistently perhaps, that if I were attacked by a painful illness I should have patience to wait for the end, and I do not think I should wish anyone near or dear to me to act otherwise'.[7] Quite clearly suicide, and perhaps even voluntary euthanasia, might in certain instances be the expression of a refusal to trust in God, an embracing of death for its own sake, a form of self-justification, a desertion to the enemy. A final act of self-determination, whether arising from courage or from fear, is substituted for a waiting patiently in hope. If such is the intrinsic character of a deliberately contrived death, it can readily be understood why it has been forbidden in the Christian tradition. But has it necessarily this character?

This is not an easy question to answer. It might be argued that, if death ought for the Christian to be a passion, something that he undergoes in utter dependence on God, then suicide and voluntary euthanasia, which make of death an action, something deliberately encompassed by a man himself, even if it is performed at the hand of another, are *ipso facto* wrong, whether they express a deliberate rejection of God or not. It is not the motive that makes the action wrong; it is wrong in itself, whatever the motive. In face of death all other considerations should give way to a simple and faithful waiting on the course of events. Certainly a man should act with prudence and concern for others in preparing for death. Equally certainly everything should be done to alleviate the pains of death. But when the time to die comes all action should give way to passive dependence upon God. Was not this the way in which Jesus himself suffered death and 'learned obedience'? Is not the unmaking of man in death the *sine qua non* of any hope of resurrection to life eternal?

Persuasive though such argument may be, sufficient perhaps to engage the concurrence of most Christians, it must not be pretended that it is conclusive. It might be replied that the reality of our ultimate dependence upon God is not impugned by the responsible exercise of our freedom of choice, even when it comes to our dying. The dialectic of freedom and dependence, of action and passion, of doing and suffering, is far more subtle than has so far been suggested. Certainly in death there is a final passion, and for victory over death we must wait in hope upon God. But does this necessarily mean that we must in all circumstances wait upon the course of events which we call dying? If the natural course of events results in my being robbed of my proper humanity through the onset of pains greater than I can bear or through the degradations of senile decay, is a decision to request that in such circumstances my life should be ended by another, before nature ends it for me, incompatible with my acknowledging my ultimate and total dependence on God? If my disintegration as a human being occurs before death, is there still any sense in speaking of my dying as either action or passion, self-determination or waiting on God?

It is sometimes asserted that a refusal to countenance voluntary euthanasia reveals a signal lack of compassion. Should we not condemn as cruel anyone who refused to put out of its misery an animal which through illness or old age had become a burden to itself? Why then refuse to human beings what we so readily grant to animals? In reply it might be said that human beings are not simply animals, and that it must not be assumed that what is fitting in our treatment of the one is necessarily fitting in our treatment of the other. This is true so far as it goes. For instance, we allow some experiments on animals which we do not allow on human beings. In this case we may be said to be less compassionate towards animals than towards human beings. Nevertheless it does not go very far. The plea for compassion is in itself a deeply human and highly moral plea which should not fall on deaf ears, whether the ears are Christian or not. However, two sets of considerations are in place.

First, the value of human life does not consist simply of a scale of pleasure and pain. Such may be the value of an animal's life. A dog's life, for example, may be valuable in so far as it is filled with doggy pleasures and devoid of doggy pains. But the value of human life consists in a variety of virtues and graces as well as in pleasure. These together constitute man's full humanity. They grow in soil in which action and passion, doing and suffering, pleasure and pain are intermixed. What a man is consists not only of what he does, but also of how he endures. A fully human life is inescapably vulnerable, as every lover knows, and even suffering may by grace be woven into the texture of a larger humanity. It is not that Christians believe that suffering is in itself a good, or that it necessarily ennobles. It may indeed destroy, and the alleviation of pain is a Christian as well as a human duty. But suffering as exposure to what is beyond one's voluntary control, suffering as undergoing, even as diminishment, is part of the pattern of becoming human. Even dying need not be simply the ebbing away of life; it may be integrated into life, and so made instrumental to a fuller life in God. To speak like this is indeed to invite the charge of idle self-deception. But the Christian hope of resurrection is admittedly a strange hope, difficult to conceive, more difficult to articulate. It is not the expectation that life as we know it will simply continue beyond the grave, a further act in the same play. It is rather the hope that faithfulness to God and man in this life, the only life that we have any obvious claims to call our own life, will find its fulfilment by God's grace in his eternal life. Thus faith in God demands fidelity here and now, not impatient anticipation of what he may have in store for us.

The second set of considerations is this. So far we have been considering death in terms of the individual's own attitude to his dying. We must also consider it in the context of the human relationships in which the individual is involved. Men exercise and achieve their humanity in interdependence. There is a movement of giving and receiving. At the beginning and at the end of life receiving predominates over and even excludes giving. But the value of human life does not depend only on its capacity to give. Love, *agape*, is the equal and unalterable regard for the value of other human beings independent of their particular characteristics. It extends especially to the helpless and hopeless, to those who have no value in their own eyes and seemingly none for society. Such neighbour-love is costly and sacrificial. It is easily destroyed. In the giver it demands unlimited caring, in the recipient absolute trust. The question must be asked whether the practice of voluntary euthanasia is consistent with the fostering of such caring and trust. Whether or not the direct killing of another person with his consent were in certain circumstances morally justifiable, it might still be the case that in principle *agape* is better expressed and more deeply nourished by the careful accompanying of a person in his dying than by any established practice of voluntary euthanasia.

It will be observed that these theological reflections have not issued in any simple or absolute moral conclusions. To some this will prove their inadequacy. To others it will accurately represent the proper nature of theological discourse. But their inconclusiveness must not be exaggerated. The arguments presented may not foreclose the moral debate in one way or the other. But they are sufficient, we believe, to show that there are strong grounds from the Christian point of view for hesitating long before admitting any exception to the principle forbidding killing human beings. The almost instinctive rejection of voluntary euthanasia by the large majority of Christians in the past and in the present is neither arbitrary nor irrational.

Our discussion of the ethical aspects of euthanasia has been deliberately set within the context of Christian beliefs about the nature and destiny of man and the creative and redemptive activity of God. There is, however, another Christian approach which we must mention; for while it does not introduce any distinctively religious considerations, it might still be claimed to be fundamental to the moral teaching of Jesus himself.

Jesus, it might be said, summed up his moral teaching concerning our behaviour towards others in the following words:

> *Therefore all things whatsoever ye would that men should do to you,*
> *do ye even so to them: for this is the law and the prophets.*[8]

This commandment, it is clear, is closely related to that in which we are bidden to love our neighbour as ourself.[9]

It is difficult in the face of these commandments to maintain either the moral position that euthanasia is always and absolutely forbidden, or the moral position that it is always permissible.

There are bound to be cases in which any of us who is honest with himself and asks 'What do I wish that men should do to me in this particular situation?' will answer 'Kill me'. We have already mentioned such unusual cases[10] in which many of us would wish to have our deaths hastened so that the manner of them might be less unbearable. Thus a direct application of the teaching of Jesus to these cases would legitimize at least some instances of euthanasia.

It certainly does not follow, however, from anything that we might wish to say about these unusual and extreme cases that euthanasia is morally legitimate in other more ordinary cases. The only person who will be tempted to say that it does so follow is one who thinks that moral principles have to be extremely simple, so that he is restricted to a choice between an absolute prohibition of euthanasia and an absolute permission of it. It is indeed useful and important to have simple moral principles as practical guides. We all think it wrong in principle to tell lies or to break promises. Even so we can also think of cases in which it would be our moral duty to tell a lie or to break a promise – for example, in order to save an innocent life. In such cases we should not be expressing any disregard of the moral importance of truth-telling or promise-keeping; we should simply be recognizing a more pressing moral claim which outweighed their undisputed value. Furthermore, it is right and proper that the Church in its teaching should lay great stress on such good and simple principles. They provide for weak and ignorant human beings an indispensable support, without which they would certainly fall into all kinds of temptations and special pleadings. But to hold such principles important, even sacred, is not incompatible with the admission that there may be highly unusual cases in which these principles ought to be overridden. That innocent human life is sacred is just such a good and simple moral principle. Indeed it is of basic moral importance. Nevertheless, there may be exceptional cases in which, as we have suggested, many of us would think it morally right that it should be overridden.

It is not clear, then, what is the precise bearing of these unusual cases upon the more common cases on which advocates of voluntary euthanasia lay most stress. Perhaps all that the unusual cases teach us is that it would be unwise to make one's conclusions about the more common cases depend on an absolute, not-to-be-questioned, moral prohibition of euthanasia. Such a position would be open to the following rebuttal: since the case for euthanasia is at least extremely plausible in these unusual cases, a case against euthanasia which rested on an absolute prohibition would be seriously weakened by what perhaps the majority of considerate people who took the words of Jesus in their natural sense would say about the unusual cases. In order to avoid this dilemma it is incumbent on the opponent of euthanasia to consider the more common cases with greater care and to classify them more accurately, in order to make sure that there are none that resemble these unusual cases in all relevant respects. This is indeed the right course for anybody, whatever his initial feelings about the question, who wants to reach a considered conclusion on it. This is in fact the course that we have attempted to follow.

It is even less clear what bearing these unusual cases have on arguments about changes in the law even if some of them are encountered in medical practice. It is not always good sense, either to make something into a crime because it is thought contrary to morality, or to make something legal because it is thought morally permissible. It is often expedient to forbid by law acts which are thought morally blameless. Such acts might include some cases of euthanasia, if, although they were held to be morally permissible, the making of them legal were likely to result in practice in the legalizing of other acts as well which the law should be seeking to prevent. All these considerations have to be taken into account in the light of particular cases. Nevertheless, it is not inappropriate at this stage to utter a word of caution. The 'good and simple principle' that innocent human life is sacred has influenced profoundly our conviction that the old and the dying should be cared for and consoled, no matter what their condition. It has been accepted by the law and by the profession of medicine. For our society to recognize any departure from it, involving consequences that we cannot predict and may not desire, would require clear, cogent and conclusive justification. For ourselves we do not think that such exists.

4

Case Histories Discussed

We return now to the four cases selected from the literature presented to the Working Party (on pages 1–3 above), and to the question already asked: had these people, and the others whose letters are published by the Voluntary Euthanasia Society, received all the help they could and should have had? It is impossible to know just what the medical situation was in each case, and, for this reason, we shall later discuss comparable cases that are more fully documented. Nonetheless, there are a few points which can be raised about the cases as presented.

Case history A is expressed in words such as 'stricken' and 'hopeless prognosis' which suggest a conviction on the part of the doctor that little or nothing can be done to help the dying patient. Cancer of the pancreas need not be a particularly distressing way to die at the age of 75. It does not usually give rise to much pain and would not appear to have done so in this case. Vomiting should be controllable, and although at the time this patient died there may not have been such a variety of drugs to relieve it, there certainly were some available which should have helped. There is, for instance, no indication in this report that the patient received morphine before the last night. Small, regular doses used at an earlier stage of her decline might have relieved discomfort and weariness, helped her to have peaceful nights and quietened her anxiety about the process of dying, if the doctor could not reassure her about this himself. The normal end for such a patient (particularly in this age group), if properly managed, is a quiet drifting into unconsciousness. It is also most unlikely that a 'modest dose of morphine' would have killed her. It certainly sounds as though she died of her disease, and that at the last she was given the relief she needed. 'The clear moral duty of the doctor' is to give both this and also proper care at every stage of such illness.

Case history B tells of an old lady whose heart was sound, appetite good and mind alert. It seems clear that it was in large part the fault of the environment that she wanted to die with so fixed and unalterable a depression.

The best way to comment on her case is perhaps to take a patient with similar problems and tell her story. Mrs L. (Case history 1 below)[1] was enabled to forget her body and its physical limitations by skilled and imaginative care, not by the hastening of her death. Anti-depressant drugs can be, and often are, of help when they are combined with diversion, changes in environment and above all, the conviction that, after all, there is still some contribution to be made in life.

Good geriatric wards and nursing homes can repeat this story many times over. The sad thing is that there are not enough of them, but the answer is to increase their number, not to reduce by 'mercy killing' the number of patients who could benefit from them.

Case history C gives more detail and raises some of the issues that are foremost in this debate. The twelve months' survival makes it unlikely that this man's disease was acute leukaemia. Had that been the case there would certainly have been an argument for giving no treatment other than the relieving of his symptoms. The likelihood, however, is that he had chronic lymphatic leukaemia, and here there is no doubt that specific treatment aimed at the disease itself can help in relieving symptoms for the remainder of the patient's life. The problem for the doctor is to decide when such specific treatment is giving diminishing returns (and perhaps increasing side effects) and should be discontinued in favour of palliative measures. The giving of blood transfusions may make a patient temporarily feel much better and more active, but the decision to give them demands careful thought and management. In this, as in other deteriorating illnesses, many small decisions have to be made, often on a day-to-day basis. Good rapport between doctor, patient, relatives and nursing staff is essential, and it would appear here that this was lacking. This illness does not inevitably entail suffering; it can be managed without distress so that such a couple is supported through the last phase of their life together. We return to the great need for adequate care in controlling mental as well as physical pain and in listening to and helping the understandably distraught relatives.

There are grounds for suspecting that in this case the wishes of the two people most concerned were not properly appreciated. We may also wonder whether this was not a case, like many others, where so-called 'curative treatment' was used without sufficient consideration for its value and appropriateness to a particular patient. The immense development of our resources in anaesthesia and in operative techniques, and the many drugs which have become available during the past twenty years or so, have not yet been balanced by judgement in using them. It does not follow that, because it is possible to do something, it is necessarily either right or kind to do it.

Case history D includes some very sad comments from a disabled and depressed person. It is a reproach to our society that such elderly people (who have been through both wars and the Depression) can feel that they are no better than burdens. It is sad also that the writer thinks that his disorders inevitably mean protracted suffering – which is apparently thought to be incapable of relief.

It is difficult to assess comments about hearing the sounds of resuscitation being carried out after attempts at suicide. Bringing round a teenager who has made a 'cry for help' attempt may include sounds one would wish had not been heard through the general ward, but that certainly does not mean the whole process is sordid.

The writer of this letter was right in saying that he would need help, but with proper care it should not be help to be killed.

The stories which we have been considering were offered as instances in which euthanasia would have been justified. Since the case for euthanasia rests on such examples as these, it is of the utmost importance to treat them seriously and in sufficient detail. An attempt is made therefore in what follows to provide some further case histories of the same character for which full clinical information is available. To keep them in proportion it must be borne in mind that they represent some of the most difficult terminal cases in institutions which admit those who are likely to suffer severe pain or other distress.[2]

Case History 1 (Contributed by a senior house-officer)

MRS. L.

Mrs. L. spent most of her 78 years in hospital, including a large part of her childhood. In spite of this she achieved marriage and some years of comparatively normal life. Her husband died when she was in her forties. She had no children and by the time we knew her she had no close relations.

Mrs. L. was born with dislocated hips and never walked normally. She was injured in the First World War and lost what movement she had. Gradually osteoarthritis affected the damaged joints, causing constant and sometimes severe pain.

29

When she came to the hospice she had been in a geriatric ward for sixteen months, receiving no active treatment as this was not considered appropriate. The consultant wrote, 'She is a lady who, although having many complaints, sometimes tempts one to feel that she makes the most of them.' After a year in the hospice this was still true.

She had much justification. She had been operated on for cataracts, and corneal opacities were gradually blurring her vision. She had a hiatus hernia, giving her severe indigestion, and also suffered from periodic attacks of jaundice. The latter caused irritation and made her feel wretched. Movement of any kind was painful because the osteoarthritis had involved many other joints besides her hips. Her dentures fitted badly and gave her a permanently sore mouth. She had frequent sore throats, sinusitis and coughs, and was subject to diarrhoea and cystitis.

Each symptom was treated as it occurred and every time a doctor saw her some fresh problem would be mentioned. Her life seemed to be just one complaint after another, each absorbing her whole attention. It is no wonder that she is recorded as saying on more than one occasion, 'I wish I was in my box'.

TREATMENT

The whole picture changed completely when the medical team was enlarged and the doctors set out to take a careful look at the needs of each of the long-stay patients. An occupational therapist also joined the team. In addition a rheumatologist was brought in to see Mrs. L. He said that nothing further could be done for her physical condition but diagnosed chronic depression and suggested that this should be treated. On anti-depressant drugs Mrs. L. improved markedly and it was soon recorded in the notes that she was 'very cheerful'. She was approached with some occupational therapy. This met with enormous resistance at first but finally the therapist found her some extra large needles which she could grip, and she was cajoled into knitting a scarf for one of the doctors which eventually reached the length of eight feet. The scarf was followed by bed-jackets, blankets, more scarves and multi-coloured tea cosies. She took to reading again and enjoyed *Lolita*. Many of her symptoms were still present, but she now accepted and made light of them. She had her down days but they no longer filled her horizon because she had stopped paying attention to them. She enjoyed life until she had an acute attack of pneumonia and died within a few days.

Discussion

It is impossible to give the exact figures, but for many patients who suffer from chronic illness or disability the element of depression is of great importance, often outweighing the physical distress itself. Such depression, rightly classed as reactive to the physical burden, nevertheless will frequently respond to specific therapy, especially when it is combined with occupation and with personal interest and satisfaction.

It is true that wards such as those in which Mrs. L. had suffered for so long are short-staffed and hard-pressed. Nevertheless it is both better medicine and a much more rewarding use of the time available to use it to listen, diagnose correctly and then treat appropriately. Many geriatric units have shown that such a positive approach reduces the overall demands made on the nursing staff.

Mrs. L. said 'I wish I was in my box.' Such remarks are not uncommon. Sometimes they are only desperate requests for attention. Often they express a desire to be rid of a burdensome existence without implying in any way a fixed determination to have life ended. Few of those who care for such patients would think that they could always interpret correctly what was being said and most of them would hesitate before taking irrevocable action on the grounds that a patient meant what he said to be taken literally. When treatment of the kind described above leads, as it so often does, to such a radical change of attitude, there can be little doubt that the burden of symptoms has been lifted and that life has again become worth living.

Case History 2 (Contributed by a consultant physician)

MISS W.

Miss W. was transferred from the hospital which had recently treated her carcinoma of the thyroid and had given her a course of radiotherapy and radioactive iodine to bony secondaries. She had an infected ulcer on her right ankle which caused her some pain.

During a conversation nearly two months after her admission she said to one of the doctors, 'Of course I believe in euthanasia.' On being asked, 'Supposing for the sake of argument you could have it, do you want it now?', she replied, 'Good gracious, no!' A longer discussion followed. Her thesis was that she did not believe in suffering either for herself or for others, but she did not consider that she was then suffering sufficiently to ask for her life to be ended. She was prepared to continue living even though she found the restricted bed-ridden situation difficult to bear.

Her ankle became more painful during the next few days and she became extremely apprehensive, fearing that any movement was going to hurt her. This fear greatly exacerbated the physical pain. While attempting to relieve her fears the doctor deliberately discussed euthanasia with her again. To the question, 'We were talking about euthanasia some time ago; would you want it now?', she replied as quickly and as spontaneously as before, 'No – I leave things to you.' She was given enough medication to ease her apprehension and to control her physical pain and became quiet and peaceful, dying about a week later.

Discussion

Requests for euthanasia must not always be taken at their face value, and it is important that the underlying meaning of such demands should be identified. Here it seems to have been a plea for the relief of pain and anxiety. Miss W. had no further need to ask for euthanasia once this relief had been given. Doctors working in this field find that they receive such requests from time to time and that, once the real question has been disentangled from what is often a somewhat confused story, there is rarely a further request. The crucial problem has been dealt with. In this case it was the doctor, not the patient, who initiated the return to the subject. By this time, however, Miss W., reassured that relief could and would be given to her, did not need to pursue it further.

Even those who think through their feelings on this subject and seriously plan such a request when they are well, are seldom consistent when they are ill. They may have full insight into their condition, as did Miss W., and still postpone a final decision. It seems fair to say that, for many who are in favour of euthanasia, a final demand remains something that is for another time, or for someone else in some hypothetical situation. For example, another patient, on being asked whether she 'wanted it now' replied 'Oh, no; only if things get worse.' She died quietly only a few days later without mentioning the subject again.

Miss W. needed skilled treatment for the control of her pain. The end of the story might well have been different if she had been allowed to suffer continuous pain or the continued expectation of pain. Once again, the need is clear for teaching and experience in this field as part of general medical and nursing education.

Case History 3 (Contributed by a nursing officer in the domiciliary service)

Mrs T.

Mrs T., a woman of 47 years, married, with three children (the youngest of whom was 6 years) was operated on for cancer of the bowel. She was not told her diagnosis, though her husband was fully informed.

Eighteen months later, having been reasonably well, she developed signs of a recurrence of the disease and was treated with radiotherapy. The treatment gave no relief and within a few months she was very ill with constant severe pain and vomiting. At about this time the husband told his wife that she was not going to get better. Her despair and hopelessness were complete, she turned her face to the wall and refused to eat, for, as she said, 'What is the point?' She made an abortive attempt to take her own life. With this effort to end her life two of her sisters, who could not bear to see her sufferings, were in sympathy. They therefore suggested to the husband that, as there were sufficient drugs in the house, they should combine them all and give them to the patient to 'end it all' and put her out of her misery. However, they disagreed and finally decided against this desperate plan.

At this moment help came in the form of skilled and understanding medical and nursing care. With proper drugs her pain and vomiting were almost entirely controlled. She remained alert and able to take stock of her situation, to voice her fears and discuss her problems. With her symptoms relieved she began to take a pride in her appearance again and to eat. For nearly twelve months more this woman led a nearly normal life with her family. She went out, did the shopping, visited friends. Eleven months later she had to be admitted to hospice, where for a brief four weeks she slipped quietly downhill, dying tranquilly after only twenty-four hours of coma.

Looking back, her husband is able to say that during that last bonus year of her life she not only enjoyed life, but gave her children the opportunity and the time to come to terms with the knowledge that she was going to die. Once her pain was relieved she never again asked for her life to be ended but, as she was dying, she repeated more than once with real satisfaction, 'At least the children are a year older.' Had the attempt at suicide been successful, these children would undoubtedly have been deeply shocked. As it was they 'took it all in their stride' (to quote their father), and there have been no traumatic effects beyond the normal grieving.

Discussion

It is likely that decisions regarding active steps to kill a patient will involve the whole family. In this case during the period of desperation some members of the family held conflicting views as to what was right. It is easy to picture the divisions and difficulties which would have arisen had the action they considered been taken.

It takes time to assimilate a painful truth or to reorganize both thinking and living in a changed set of circumstances. 'It takes a long time to know what it means to be a widow, it takes a long time to prepare oneself to die.'[3] This is part of the pain of bereavement. Sudden deaths are frequently followed by marked distress and feelings of guilt and self-reproach and are often more difficult for the survivors to come to terms with than bereavement after expected deaths. Suicide may lead to particularly intractable problems for those left behind.[4]

Mrs. T. required strong analgesics, including narcotic drugs, over many months. They neither lost their effectiveness nor damped her strong personality. Their skilled use enabled her to live an active life until shortly before her death. They did much to give her and her family the extra time they all needed. Her husband was taught by the doctor and nurses in an out-patient and domiciliary department of a hospice to regulate the dose of her medication according to her needs, which might change from day to day. Because of this careful assessment she never required any substantial increase in dose, and her husband had a great sense of achievement in helping her in this way.

Case History 4 (Contributed by a senior registrar and a nursing auxiliary)

Mr J.

A man of 75 had a total laryngectomy for cancer of the larynx unresponsive to radiotherapy. Healing after the laryngectomy was slow and a fistula developed. His condition deteriorated, and a recurrence was noted in the posterior wall of the wound. This was treated by a cytotoxic preparation, methotrexate (an anti-cancer drug). The treatment was not successful, and with the onset of increasingly severe difficulty in swallowing he was admitted to hospital. Owing to his age and frailty he was treated palliatively, with drugs given to control his pain and thirst. He would almost certainly have died peacefully within a few days. However, although the doctors were against it, *the son* (not the patient) was insistent that a gastrostomy should be performed, and in order to get his way he arranged for the patient to be transferred to another hospital where the doctors were willing to operate. Subsequently gastrostomy feeds were given four-hourly by a tube passed directly through the abdominal wall into the stomach. To begin with, all went well and Mr J. was at home, reasonably active. However, after three months he became too weak to be cared for any longer by his family and was admitted for terminal care. The patient was noted to be agitated at times and tended to be difficult when fed. He slowly deteriorated, having periods of drowsiness and faecal incontinence. Some two months after admission one nurse wrote in his notes, 'The patient for the past couple of weeks has been trying to convey something to me when I fed him. I knew what he was trying to say, I think, but I couldn't be certain. Today when I went to give the 2.00 p.m. feed he said quite clearly, with a look of panic and desperation on his face, "Please, no more feeds". He was waving his hands and holding on to me almost begging me to stop. (On previous occasions he had seemed to upset feeds deliberately.) I asked him if he wanted to die and his face changed to a peaceful resignation and he nodded. I gave him the feed. He half-heartedly tried to stop me but he had become weak with all the agitation.' After discussion between the doctor, the sister and the nurses, the four-hourly feeds were discontinued. Adequate sedation to control thirst was given, and the patient became more peaceful. He died five days later.

Discussion (This case resembles Case History C above, page 2, discussed on page 28)

Technical medicine, which is essential for the successful treatment of acute and curable conditions, all too easily becomes a machine producing inappropriate and indeed harmful treatment once the disease is irreversible. It can rarely be more than a prolongation of an already distressful dying for a patient such as Mr. J. However, it should be noted that in this case the first group of doctors were ready to ease Mr. J.'s dying without performing such an operation and it was the family who pressed for it and found a second group who responded to their wishes. One does not know how fully the gastrostomy was explained and discussed with the patient nor whether every effort had been made earlier to help the family to come to terms with his inevitable death.

Case History 5 (Contributed by a senior house-officer)

Miss P.

Miss P., aged 85, was admitted to hospital after a severe stroke. After some months her condition had improved to some extent but, as she remained confined to a wheel chair, often confused and sometimes incontinent, it was decided that, much as they wished to, her two elderly sisters could not care for her at home. She was therefore transferred to a hospice for long-term care.

Despite regular physiotherapy her legs never regained their strength. When, in her confusion, she tried them out when the nurses' backs were turned, she sustained a black eye and other bruises. Her incontinence became worse and a catheter was inserted. On one occasion she said, 'You'll never turn me out, will you?' On another she wept and pleaded to go home, against all reasoning. Drugs were never very successful in controlling her confusion. Twenty months after her first stroke she had another and died the following day without regaining consciousness.

Discussion

The bare facts of Miss P.'s story are bleak. But there is another, more subtle, side to the tale. To the last she was adored by her sisters and she would watch the clock for their daily arrival. It was her happiness and theirs during these visits, and the close relationship which she formed with two of the nurses, which first alerted me to look more closely at her. Her mind might be damaged but she was both giving and receiving in relationship with those around her. Her life did not end with the first stroke; it had meaning to its natural end.

Only those in close contact with her could really see Miss P. A more distant observer might feel that her true desire must surely have been to have her life brought painlessly to an end. Visitors to long-stay wards can expect to make only superficial judgements, not only concerning distress but also concerning the quality of life there. We cannot emphasize sufficiently the impact that seeing the seriously ill has on healthy people. This shock reaction often causes them to read into the minds of patients thoughts which are merely projections of their own emotional reactions.

Case History 6 (Contributed by a staff nurse)

Tony

Tony was admitted to a hospice suffering from motor neurone disease, a neurological illness at present incurable, which affects the muscles progressively but has no effect on

37

sensation or mental alertness. During a two and a half months' stay he gained confidence in his now limited capacity, and his wife was able to change to part-time work. After trial weekends he returned home indefinitely on the understanding that he would be readmitted immediately should the need arise. Seven and a half months later they both decided that they could manage no longer. This time together had been good but, as his wife said, 'What we have together now is so splendid that I would hate to jeopardize it by becoming too tired to cope – and we do get frightened sometimes.' On re-admission he could still do a little for himself and enjoyed reading and music. Over the course of two years he became progressively dependent upon others and more and more easily fatigued. Gradually his tape-recorder, his wheelchair outings and even long conversations became too much for him. He lost his voice, but his wife and several members of staff learned to lipread what he said, and he waited with endless patience while they persevered.

As Tony became aware that he was not going to recover from his illness, he began to talk about dying; he was not afraid of death, but of *how* he would die. As swallowing became more of an effort, so his fear of choking to death increased. He spoke of euthanasia and asked, 'Why should I go on living in this way?' While we could sympathize with these feelings and certainly did not want Tony to suffer any more, at the same time the thought of euthanasia was impossible for any of us to contemplate. *Who would give the fatal injection?* When would we know that the time had really come? Tony, well aware of *our* feelings on the subject, could appreciate the difficulties. He was ambivalent about this desire, for just as frequent were his requests that anyone suffering from a cold or sore throat should not go too near him. He would say, 'I could not throw off a cold; it might prove fatal!' We also learned that he had asked his wife while he was still at home to give him an overdose of sleeping pills at a time when he could no longer reach out for them for himself. She could not bring herself to do this. They discussed it and agreed that, while they could perhaps take an overdose for themselves, neither of them could contemplate giving one to the other.

Tony was deeply involved in all that was going on around him. Even though he was unable to talk so that they could hear him, other patients included him in their conversations. In the next bed was a young man with multiple sclerosis who was also blind. Although the two could communicate only through others, a close friendship developed between them. In spite of all his physical disabilities and many frustrations Tony was still able to be concerned about others and talk with wit and directness. He would give a warm smile to any who spoke with him, especially when they finally battled through to understand what he was conveying to them.

Throughout his long illness Tony's wife visited him regularly and frequently. She would sit close to him, chatting, reading, feeding him; and then before leaving she would settle him down comfortably for the night in a deft and capable way which none of the nurses could match; she knew just how he liked to be. From what had been a rather unstable marriage before Tony's illness there grew an unusually close and loving relationship. This gave them strength and confidence to go on together until Tony died peacefully in his sleep. He had by then become confident that he would not be allowed to choke, and when he had a massive pulmonary embolus he slipped easily into unconsciousness and died in a few hours.

Discussion

Such a disease results in great frustration for the patient. Less obviously, perhaps, it frequently results in the kind of achievements that are described above. The nurses, the doctors and, above all, his wife found that Tony drew out the best that was in them. They also found that in the interchange he was giving them more than they were giving him, laborious as his care may have looked to an outsider. The possibilities of such achievements must be set against the negative attitude of those who can see only pointless and hopeless suffering in such situations and wish only to turn their backs on them. Tony left behind him memories to give courage and firmness. His care involved many people in hard work and concern which no one grudged. To have given a lethal injection during one of his depressed moments would have left doubts which could never have been resolved.

Tony's ambivalent thoughts about euthanasia are typical. One moment a patient may express a definite wish for it; the next make some comment (as he often did) which shows that his desire to avoid death and to go on living is still strong. Some change their opinions completely. Another young man, also with motor neurone disease, was admitted into the bed opposite Tony. On one occasion he said to the night sister, 'If I ever got like that chap I'd want to do something to myself.' In fact, when he finally reached almost exactly the same condition in his turn, he found that his feelings had changed and that the experience from inside was not what it appeared to the onlooker. To one of the doctors he said, 'I can't see round the next bend, but I know it will be all right.' He found, as he said, that what he had experienced and what he had seen in others was a 'bringing-together illness. In this kind of life the complexities fall away; what is left is what matters.'

It is not only in the patient that character can grow and the mind and spirit become stronger. This is often true for the family also: the young wife above has remarried and brought to her new life the strengths she found in the years with Tony.

Case History 7 (Contributed by a consultant physician)

Mrs D.

Mrs D., aged 49, had an operation for cancer of the colon. Four months later she was given a course of radiotherapy for a recurrence of the disease on her abdominal wall. A few weeks later, with pain, a discharging wound and a bedsore, she was transferred by her treatment hospital to a hospice for terminal care. She was given several courses of antibiotics, which, by controlling the infection surrounding the growth, removed both the offensiveness of the discharge and most of her pain. Mild drugs were then sufficient to relieve any residual discomfort for the remaining months of her life. It could be argued that the antibiotics possibly prolonged her life as well as controlled the distressing infection. It is difficult to judge, but they certainly made her much more comfortable. The bedsore also became painless and gradually healed.

She was soon able to get up in a wheelchair and became busy with occupational therapy. She took an active part in the life of the ward and was able to go home for an occasional weekend. Her son came on leave from overseas, and she enjoyed meeting his new girl friend.

Five months after admission, and a few days before her death, Mrs D. began to get confused. One of the fears which she expressed was a dread of being given an injection, and she had to be reassured several times that we would not give her anything without her consent. At this stage I had a long conversation with her husband. He had been kept fully in the picture throughout her illness but had been telling her that she was going to get better. On this occasion he said, 'If it was hopeless from the start, was there any need to go on? Could we not have made the end come more quickly?' He appeared to appreciate, if not to agree, that such a course would have been neither possible nor lawful. During the discussion he was told that she would be given a tranquillizer to help allay her confused anxieties. A small dose helped Mrs D. into a deep sleep. Two hours later, when I went again to see her, Mr D. was sitting with her. He said, 'She has not moved since you gave her that last tablet.' I told him that the effect of this particular drug would almost certainly wear off after about four hours. Indeed, after five hours she woke, quite alert and more rational. She said to her husband, 'You have been deceiving me.' He repeated this to me, adding, 'She was wandering.' She woke a second time after some hours, and then lapsed into unconsciousness and died peacefully a few hours later. She never had to have an injection.

Discussion

This story raises some of the common practical issues that arise concerning patients dying of malignant diseases. In the first place, Mr. D. speaks for a large number of relatives when he refers to his wife's illness as 'hopeless'. Doctors are reported as saying this, and while the word itself may often be a kind of shorthand used by the family to sum up what they have been told in a lengthy and careful discussion of the prognosis, too often it is a true report of what they have been told and the manner in which the information has been given.

Mr. D. questions whether steps should not have been taken to 'end it all more quickly' even though he has seen his wife free from pain, alert and cheerful for the past five months. But he is the one who asks, not his wife. Furthermore, he has been determined throughout that she should not be told the nature of her illness, while she, in her turn, has all along appeared not to wish to look at what is happening and its implications. But a patient will not be sufficiently informed to make a request for a quicker ending unless she knows the likely outcome. Although patients are frequently realistic about their illness and show much courage in facing it, many families do their best to 'protect' them and should voluntary euthanasia be legalized, such a dilemma would not be uncommon. Either Mr. D. must ask someone to tell his wife that her case is 'hopeless' – and few doctors would be happy to take such an initiative and impose information on her which she has been avoiding – or else Mr. D. must face the fact that it is his wish, not hers, that is being considered. That is, he (like many who ask for 'release' for others) must recognize that he is in fact speaking of involuntary, not of voluntary euthanasia. It is too easy to attribute one's feelings to others.

Mrs. D. was a fighter. All doctors have seen unexpected recoveries even at this stage and would hesitate to say that there was no hope of further improvement in any particular patient. Such remissions are admittedly rare, but there is another more disturbing possibility, which would occur more frequently. Mrs. D., even if she had been told that death was inevitable within a few months and that she could be offered a 'quick release', would not necessarily have accepted this fact, nor agreed with the solution suggested to her. Where then would she turn? Home to the husband she knew must have discussed this course, and who in any case could not give her the nursing she needed? Back to the acute treatment hospital who had already suggested admission to this new place which made such an alarming proposal? She would hardly feel secure with anyone who had been involved with such a suggestion, nor would she again believe that those who had offered such a solution would, if she refused it, then do all they could to enable her to live out her life as long and as well as possible.

Mrs. D. was not unusual in having a fear of injections, nor in being suspicious of medications. There is no doubt that there are people whose peace of mind and trust in those caring for them, never perhaps very secure, have been undermined by discussion of the subject of euthanasia in the media. These fears would be far more widespread if it were known that euthanasia of any kind had been legalized. It has been argued that people would know whether they had signed a form, discussed the subject, or made any sort of request of this nature; but those who are ill, especially among the elderly, do not easily trust their memories and all too easily become uncertain of the motives of those around them. Those who are constantly in touch with these patients will recognize in Mrs. D. common suspicions and insecurities which could place intolerable burdens on patients and indirectly on those who care for them.

It is often reported by relatives and by doctors themselves that they 'help patients over the last hurdle'. This has been termed a form of euthanasia and considered to be at least tacit approval of a final deliberate overdose.[5] This story illustrates one way in which this view may arise and be a complete misconception. If the doctor had not gone back to discuss the treatment of this patient, Mr. D. could easily have said that the tablets had been given to kill her. (He may indeed still have done so.) Mrs. D.'s death is most unlikely to have been hastened by a small dose of a well-known tranquillizer (chlorpromazine 25 mg.), but there is little doubt that her end came much more peacefully as a result. Those who use the phrase 'helping over the last hurdle' frequently mean no more than this. They have been continuing the practice of good medicine and taking responsibility for easing the last hours of a patient's life. Families who report that 'the doctor then gave her something . . .' must often be reporting their interpretation of such a course of action. It need hardly be emphasized that it is important that doctors and nurses explain what they are doing.

Legislation concerning a 'right to die', with all the procedures and safeguards which would be called for, could well hinder proper terminal care. A legal necessity for further consultation, the signing of documents, etc. would both hinder and delay action often needed promptly. It could also impose traumatic decisions on both patient and family. This would gratuitously increase suffering and make doctors less able to carry out responsible treatment to ease the act of dying and to teach this skill to others.

5

Further Medical Considerations

Making clinical judgements

It is already being taught[1] and frequently discussed in meetings of students and younger doctors (e.g. in such bodies as the London Medical Group and the Society for the Study of Medical Ethics), that clinical judgement includes the responsibility of a doctor, in his pursuit of cure and of resuscitation, to decide at what stage it is in the real interests of a patient for him to step back and halt the process. His duty then is to relieve the pains of dying. It cannot be too strongly emphasized that this is a question of clinical duty, not one of law.

Moreover, just as the process of resuscitation is the work of a team, so too is the work of giving relief and peace to the mortally ill. In order to make these decisions and to give this relief, the doctor should consult with all who can provide relevant information concerning his patient. First among these are the nurses, who are the closest to the patient and who know him and the family, in most instances, far better than the doctor can. These consultations should include some attempt to discover the views of the patient himself. No statements made in the past by a patient can ever take the place of the patient's communication with his doctor. Good terminal care must include constant listening to the patient's own point of view, for a personal rapport is always of greater value than a piece of paper dating from an earlier time in the patient's life when he may well have had a different attitude.

What is appropriate treatment for one patient may well be inappropriate for another. No doctor claims that he will make infallible judgements, but that is no excuse for refusing to make decisions. 'Curative' treatment is sometimes continued regardless of its relevance because no decision has been made. A family, who are pressing for 'anything possible to be done', may not be told that the likely result of any further operation or treatment will be merely to prolong distress for the patient. The question is not 'to treat or not to treat?' It is *how* to treat. To say that every active intervention possible must be pursued

45

to the bitter end is as wrong and as heartless as to say, 'There is nothing more to be done', and to abandon a patient. It is entirely misleading to call decisions to cease curative treatment 'negative euthanasia'; they are part of good medicine, and always have been.

Treating the elderly

Much of the literature published about euthanasia concerns the elderly sick and expresses either fears that treatment will be pursued without regard for their wishes or the conviction that they are certain to end their days in long-stay geriatric units which may leave much to be desired. Further, on the one hand, complaints are heard about batteries of tests being inflicted on ill, elderly patients, and, on the other, there is often a negative or even nihilistic attitude to treating them at all. 'But treatment, prognosis and planning for the patient's future is dependent on diagnostic accuracy.'[2] As is apparent from the case histories, requests to be allowed to die may be expressed in the course of an illness. However, modern geriatric methods, based on accurate diagnosis, frequently result in recovery, significant improvement, or the overcoming of major disabilities. When this happens it is the rule for patients to change their minds and no longer to express the wish to die. Many have acknowledged this change of heart and are grateful that their wish to die was not granted. The request to die should not be taken at its face value at the stage of an illness when morale is at its lowest and nursing and drug therapy have not had their chance. Consistent requests often stem from social conditions, and also from the feeling on the part of patients that they are now a burden upon those around them. The need for home support and the provision of help of all kinds (including financial assistance) for hard-pressed families is often as great as that for medical treatment.

'There exists a very small minority of patients who have apparently decided for themselves that their time has come and that they now wish to depart. They seldom express it in words and they are not apparently confused, but their negative actions, refusal to eat or drink or to cooperate in any treatment, make their intention plain. It is usually pointless to try to prevent their behaving in this way and few geriatric physicians would seriously attempt to do so.'[3] These people, we note, do not say 'Kill me'; their unexpressed wish is 'Let me die'. They can be, and commonly are, made comfortable if they become distressed or restless, and this leaves them free to change their minds at any time.

When potentially remediable illnesses occur in otherwise active old people, they should be treated actively. With diseases that have a poor prognosis it is questionable whether any except symptomatic treatment should be attempted. Once again accurate diagnosis is important in making this distinction. Elective operations of various kinds can be fully justified at almost any age for the relief of immobility, deformity, pain, discomfort or significant social disability. By contrast, the use of emergency resuscitation methods for cardiac arrest and other crises seldom seems justified in the elderly either on ethical grounds or on the results obtained. To discuss the question before-hand, with all who may be concerned, whether or not to resuscitate a given patient in the event of such a crisis, is preferable to setting a general age limit beyond which resuscitation should be withheld. All patients are different and these decisions must be individual and carefully arrived at. Most geriatric departments should be able to offer a high priority for admission to dying patients who need it. 'There comes a time even in the most dramatic lethal illnesses when it is right finally to withdraw the life-support system, remove the tubes, the infusion apparatus or oxygen mask and let the patient depart privately, peacefully and with dignity.'[4]

Most people fear mental deterioration far more than they fear death. It is correct, although it may be small comfort, to inform those who fear greatly any loss of mental capacity that older people can and do adapt to changes in both mental and physical powers. Many disorientated and even demented people do not seem to be unhappy or distressed, and some are certainly quite the reverse. Insight into the change that is taking place is often lost at an early stage and, while this may seem to be a disaster in the eyes of the younger beholder, it is not so clear-cut a tragedy to the person concerned. Work with older patients reveals that, when prowess, activity and independence are diminished, life does not necessarily lose its meaning. A protected life, with sympathetic family or nurses (and there are more of both than some seem to think), may be a natural and acceptable sequel to life's activities. Even incontinence, the greatest dread of many, need be no more offensive nor humiliating at the end of life than it is at the beginning. It is certainly true that there are too many poorly housed and inadequately staffed long-stay units and too few good ones, but the answer to that is surely clear. It may also be emphasized that the more family and friends encourage independence and social importance, the less likely are mental powers to fail. 'Senility' is sadly often a social disaster rather than an organic clinical condition and may be a retreat from isolation and unpleasant reality. To think merely in terms of easing such people out of life because of society's failure would be to encourage still further the present tendency to seek easy and selfish ways out of all problems.

Anyone who has spent time with 'senile' patients where they are lovingly cared for has seen how often they have much love both to give to, and evoke from, those who care for them. The happiness of such wards, not unlike that of some communities for the mentally handicapped, has an important perspective to offer to a society preoccupied with materialism and an over-intellectual approach to life.

Life Before Death

Life Before Death[5] is a study which gives a picture of the way our society cared for a group of people, many of whom were old and many of whom were sick for most of the year before their death, although it included a small number who had died suddenly without any previous illness. It is based upon interviews with relatives and friends of 785 people, a random sample of adults who had died, and it was carried out in several selected areas in England. It is the fullest survey of this kind that has been carried out and tells us more of how people are in fact dying than anything that has been attempted before. It bears out what had been suggested in previous, smaller studies by Aitken-Swan (1959), Marie Curie Foundation (1952), Rees (1972) and Wilkes (1965)[6] Previous studies have concentrated upon cancer deaths; Ann Cartwright has included all causes of death. In fact 20.6 per cent died of cancer, 52.4 per cent of various types of circulatory disease (including coronary artery occlusion and cerebral vascular accidents) and 14.8 per cent of respiratory illness. Three-quarters of them needed some help during the last year of their lives, and most of their care devolved on relatives and friends. This work reveals many gaps in the present services and shows that there are still insufficient beds in hospitals or appropriate homes, particularly for old people needing long-term nursing care. The Community Services were often found to be deficient; for example, 'nearly two-thirds of the district nurses felt that they would like to be able to give more time to those with terminal illness.' The Home Help Service was not sufficiently staffed to give all the assistance that was needed, and housing for the elderly and sick at home was often unsatisfactory. 'All these,' says Ann Cartwright, 'require money. Central and local government need to be persuaded that investment in them is worthwhile. The pay-off is death with greater dignity.'[7]

The study revealed loopholes and gaps in the coordination of the services, difficulties concerning admission to and discharge from hospital and failure of communication. Much may be hoped from the re-organization of services, and perhaps in particular from the attachment of district nurses and health visitors to group practices, a process which has been accelerated since the survey was finished. But we should all be deeply disturbed about the need which has been revealed in such careful detail.

One of the study's most disconcerting findings was the high proportion of symptoms for which apparently no one had been consulted. Over half of those suffering from an offensive smell and of those with loss of bladder but not bowel control were said not to have sought help from any professional person even though the doctor was visiting. On the other hand, in spite of the heavy care often involved, it is heartening to read that Ann Cartwright was impressed by the volume and intensity of care given by relatives and friends to many of those who had died. Much of the last year for most of the group was spent at home, and 40 per cent died there. Fifty-nine per cent of these people were aged 70 or over and there can be no doubt from these figures that families are still prepared to go to great lengths to care for those who are dying. Many still guard their independence and do not wish for outside help. This can never be forced on anyone, but, even so, continued independence with added community support should have been offered as an option. They should at least have been told what help was available.

The difference that skilled support at home can make was illustrated by Sheila Hancock's description of the contrast between her mother's death and that of her husband when she spoke at the opening session of the Department of Health and Social Security conference on the Care of the Dying in 1973.[8]

When looking after her mother she knew nothing of the equipment which could be made available, nor of the Marie Curie Foundation nurses. No one told her that she was entitled to the help of a district nurse and, as she said, 'You do not, as an actress, know how to deal with bedsores and enemas and suppositories and things like that. I could not 'phone my general practitioner at all hours of the night; there was no 24-hour service as far as I knew; in fact, I was often left in the middle of the night with my mother in absolute agony, not knowing where to turn'. A month after her mother's death her husband was found to have inoperable oesophageal cancer. On this occasion she received the help she needed and the story could hardly have been more different: 'My husband and I went to the theatre two days before he died, because his drugs were dosed in such a way that he never became a vegetable, and his life, even though he was consumed with the disease at the end, was always worth living.'

Successful pain control of this kind is possible for many more patients than are yet receiving it. It could be widespread and it is already being taught extensively, but it has not yet reached far enough. The amount of pain that may be suffered by patients at home, noted by Cartwright, has also been found by Parkes, who has carried out a survey among 250 families all living in two London boroughs, where a patient had died of cancer. This bears out many of Cartwright's findings. Twenty-seven per cent of spouses, where the patient had died at home, reported that the patient had severe pain which was given inadequate relief.[9] A hospice is now operating a home-care programme in this district and is being called on frequently for advice in pain control and for support for the family. Informal discussions and occasional conferences are also held with the local family doctors and district nurses. Similar programmes are developing in other districts, in most cases based on a hospice or similar home. Several regional conferences followed the Department of Health and Social Security's conference referred to above.

Thus the scene is gradually changing. More facts, such as those quoted above, are becoming available, more money has been allocated for the aged and chronically sick, and the re-organization of the community services is beginning to fill some of the gaps which have been revealed. It is to this process of fact-finding and consequent improvement of practical care and help that effort and attention should be directed if the large number of people known to suffer in their dying are to be reached and relieved.

At the same time, these studies suggest that a law to legalize voluntary euthanasia would reach little of this distress. It would appear indeed that for most of the people concerned the effect would be adverse, directing attention away from their real needs and, more likely than not, making them feel a social pressure to think of themselves as unwanted citizens. It is not always recognized for how few people at present this question is of any relevance. Only a small proportion of the population of this country plan ahead for their deaths to the extent of making a will. People are surely just as unlikely to set about signing forms of the kind that is suggested unless some form of pressure were to be put upon them with the consequences discussed earlier in this report.[10] The relatives questioned in the Parkes survey were not asked their views on euthanasia, but in what were often long interviews they had ample opportunities to express any views they might have had. The interviewer who carried out the work reports that only one or two in the survey mentioned the matter at all. 'It is fair to say that it did not appear to be a live issue for them.'[11]

Medical provision is to a large extent a reflection of general social concern and it is important that the general public should be adequately informed and reminded of their responsibilities as members of a community which includes the weak and handicapped as well as the active and productive. Many of the families approached in the survey experienced little interest or help from anyone outside their immediate circle. Gorer has reported the isolation of the bereaved.[12] Yet, in spite of general indifference, it is not difficult to arouse understanding and even action in individual, particular situations. It is important that people should both be informed of need and be encouraged to respond to it.

It would seem just as important that they should know that proper care and support could achieve a gentle, dignified death for all, and that fears of inevitable pain should be unjustified. If every broadcast programme and every article in the press on the subject of death and dying could concentrate on the need for still more widespread provision of the kind of care that is increasingly available, rather than upon the call for voluntary euthanasia, it would do much to help the great majority. All of us are going to die. Confidence that such provision will be there when the time comes will be enough to reassure most people, who in any case prefer not to look towards their death and are unlikely to sign any forms concerning it.

If such care were always available, it is likely that some of those who do wish their deaths to be hastened would feel like the patient referred to in a letter recently received at a hospice: 'X found real friends, real peace and real happiness during his last weeks, and his wife, while gratefully handing over the immediate responsibilities of his care and comfort, always felt fully involved and never isolated during his hospitalization. I think you might be interested to hear that, as a friend and a member of the medical profession, I saw him become once more his old relaxed self with you and achieving your objective of alertness with minimal pain. During one of the many long talks we had peacefully in the ward he told me he had quite reversed his ideas on euthanasia – not because he was now near death and clinging to life from fear – but because he considered himself and his wife fortunate to bring life to a close in a dignified way and to be able to say those things that otherwise might have been left unsaid.'

As another patient put it, 'When I was in the teaching hospital I was acutely uncomfortable and could hardly bear myself at all, and I asked various friends of mine who were doctors if they would help me if I wanted to die and whether they would give me something, and a couple of them said Yes; but fortunately I never did ask for it. I think that fairly soon afterwards I heard that I was coming here, and it seemed to relieve the necessity. In a way I think I'm a very good argument against euthanasia. If I had accepted it I would have missed many weeks of really enjoyable life. I should hate to have done that.'

Medical education

Ann Cartwright ends her book with a plea for changes in medical education and orientation. Only 2 per cent of her sample had died in teaching hospitals. 'This suggests not only that doctors are rarely confronted with death during their training, but also that they do not see much of the illnesses which cause death . . . The skills inculcated and admired are diagnosis and specific therapy. Yet the common medical needs today are for the relief of chronic and common conditions.'[13]

It is indeed no wonder that the doctor so often feels helpless and awkward in this situation and stays only briefly at the bedside of the dying patient, thinking that there is nothing he can do. And yet it can be shown daily in active geriatric units, in centres for terminal care and in homes visited by experienced family doctors, that it is possible to set out to diagnose and treat the causes of distress in incurable conditions and to apply specific therapy to relieve them.

A great deal of work has been carried out over recent years which has shown that distress can be relieved, both in hospital and in the patient's own home.[14] Previously a neglected subject, the treatment of chronic and terminal pain is being considered, written of and taught.[15] One hospice, which has a teaching department, sends staff out to give nearly 200 lectures and talks in a year and welcomes some 2,000 visitors and nearly 100 residents, usually in multi-disciplinary groups. Another has had visits from 400 medical students in a year. Others have regular teaching sessions for the students in medical schools.

Many post-graduate centres, local medical societies and refresher courses in all the disciplines concerned, all over the country, deal with this subject regularly. A section on 'drugs for the dying' has for several years appeared in one of the textbooks of pharmacology.[16] Terminal care is at last becoming a part of medical teaching and this subject recurs in many lectures and conferences organized by students themselves (see the programme of the London Medical Group).

Research is confirming that patients do not have to wait until their last hours for the relief of a dose of morphine, but that narcotic drugs can be used for months without detriment to the patient's personality or even activities.[17] This is not 'protracted euthanasia', or a 'living death', as it has been called, but a way of enabling someone to live actively up to the moment of his death. There are many other, less powerful, drugs and many ways of controlling pain, both for patients with cancer (the disease most commonly mentioned in the euthanasia literature) and for those with other diseases which can also cause great and prolonged distress. There is also much knowledge concerning the control of other symptoms, including nausea, vomiting, breathlessness and depression. Technical resourcefulness can be combined with awareness of the individual patient's emotional and social needs and those of his family.

There are many misapprehensions concerning terminal pain and its relief. The general public fear that the pain in incurable illness, particularly cancer, is inevitable and cannot be relieved. Much has been made of this in the euthanasia literature. It is said that depressed consciousness must always accompany adequate relief and that all strong analgesics (pain-controlling drugs) have a decreasing effectiveness. The dangers of drug dependence (addiction) are feared by professional workers as well as by the public. Many appear to believe that a patient with terminal pain will need escalating doses of any drug used to relieve it and that this itself will eventually kill him. This has been described as 'protracted euthanasia'. It is implied that many doctors practise this already as their only alternative.

These fears must be allayed; for in fact the pain of terminal cancer can be fully relieved. In most cases effective drugs, available to any practitioner, can be given by mouth throughout a patient's illness. For a few patients drugs will have to be given by injection and usually these will be required for a short time only. All these drugs should be given regularly as routine medication and will prevent pain from occurring at all. This can be so for all but a very small number of cases (see

Appendix 1). The patient will then not make his pain worse by his fear and tension and does not have to keep asking for relief. An ever-increasing number of drugs is also available to enhance the action of analgesics or, just as important, to treat other symptoms. They can be used in combination with analgesics. Records of large groups of patients treated at home as well as in hospital have shown that for the majority small doses of analgesics remain effective and that, where a large dose is required, it does *not* lose its effect nor does it necessarily depress consciousness. There is no 'routine' dose. There is only the constantly re-assessed dose for each individual patient, who can in this way be given relief to the end of his life. Giving the right drugs correctly is not tantamount to killing a patient slowly. The relief of pain itself may well lengthen life: it will certainly enhance it.

It may be difficult, but it has been shown that it is not impossible, to do this in a general hospital ward; and a most welcome trend is the interchange and discussion which are being developed between teaching hospitals and hospices. Allied to this is interest in several areas in the United Kingdom in setting up either a part of a hospital or a team with a special interest and experience in such work. There is now no excuse for the unrelieved distress that is reported. Those who despair of giving relief and think that pain is inevitable should come and see what is being done.

A terminal illness can be transformed into a time for which everyone concerned is grateful. As the mother of a 21-year-old put it in a letter, 'At one time during S.'s illness, when he was desperately ill in hospital and in great agony, my only thought and prayer was that he should be spared further suffering; and I think I even actively wanted him to die to be at peace, his agony was so terrible to see, and so little was done to relieve him. I know that, if anyone had told me then they could give him an injection which would end his pain, and also his life, I would have been tempted to say "yes". But I know we would have been wrong. It was soon after this that we came into contact with you and were able to fight with knowledge for what we knew was right for him. He did have pain again but not so terrible, and during those last four months he found a marvellous calm and acceptance, and the grace of God led him to a peaceful end which was an example to all who knew him. It has convinced me that it is never right to take a life – we do not know how God will work in what time is left.'

If students are to learn something of the problems of illness in other than purely technical terms they need to be encouraged to work as members of interdisciplinary teams. The care for a dying person and his family must be a shared work, and involves the nurses, the social workers and the chaplain; perhaps also the volunteer, the ward orderly and the receptionist. Any one of them may assume greater importance than the doctor for a particular family, for he is not automatically the leader of the team in every situation. Experience for students of various disciplines to work together during their training, and participation in formal and informal case discussions, important as they are in every branch of medical care, are essential in this field. Such a team will soon find that the family, the patient himself (and often other patients in the ward), and the workers of the relevant community services are also part of the group.

It has been noted that few families talk directly with dying patients about their illness. This may lead to much sorrow and bitterness after bereavement[18] and it is important that the clinician should learn to listen to what the patient and his family are struggling, often incoherently, to tell him about their predicament. Much mutual and painful effort may be required in order to help a family to move from an entrenched position of denial to one where the fatal illness can be directly faced. As it is, people are left alone with the very truth from which everyone around them is persuading himself they are being protected, and even the family doctor does not find it easy to reach a position of mutual frankness with a patient or his family. Here again the team is important. Both family and patient are likely to speak of their anxieties with the nurses, the students, the junior doctors, in fact everyone before they are able (if they ever are) to speak to the consultant who never appears without his entourage. Progress in real meeting may be made if the other members of the team can be encouraged to share information with the doctor who has the final responsibility for giving it to the patient.

Patients do not criticize doctors who try to open up communication on the subject of mortal illness,[19] and much mental pain is eased when doctors learn how to listen.

We do not know where the consequences of legislation permitting voluntary euthanasia would end; we do know that possibilities of relief already exist. Research and planning in this whole field and, above all, teaching for all the professions involved are called for if people are to die more easily and with greater dignity.

The positive medical approach is to work for this and at the same time see that everything possible is done to ease the passage of the 'hard cases' now and in the future (when there should be many fewer of them). Those who believe that any legislation in this area would lead to an unpredictable amount of suffering, and almost certainly much abuse, have a responsibility to work towards a situation in which no one should ever have to ask for release because of unrelieved distress. It has been shown that this is possible; the thrust is now to make relief available to all.

6

Legal Considerations

In order to understand the attitude of the law towards euthanasia we must first consider how the law regards killing in general and its understanding of the principle of the sanctity of life. We should also examine how it assesses the obligations of health professionals towards the care of the dying and to sustain human life.

The sanctity of human life is recognized in the law in a number of ways. The European Convention on Human Rights states that 'everyone's right to life shall be protected by law. No one shall be deprived of his life intentionally save in the execution of a sentence of a court . . .'[1] This commitment to protection from unlawful killing is seen in the law of homicide. It is also demonstrated by the existence of a system to ensure that deaths are reviewed so that any wrongdoing would be discovered.

The killing of a human being is something that English law regards as *prima facie* wrong and certainly as an event which requires investigation. It is the function of the coroner to identify, on behalf of society, the cause of death so that anything requiring further inquiry can be brought to light. The coroner must be informed of deaths occurring during an operation, under the effects of an anaesthetic, or where a doctor has not attended the deceased during their last illness. It is not always necessary for an inquest to be held, but it is obligatory where there is reason to suspect that there has been a violent or unnatural death or a sudden death from an unknown cause. It was the coroner who advised the doctor treating Tony Bland, the young man crushed in the disaster at the Hillsborough stadium, that it would be prudent to seek a court declaration of the legality of the withdrawal of life-sustaining care.

This firm rejection of the acceptability of killing does not prevent the law distinguishing between unlawful deaths. A range of different offences, with differing penalties available to the courts, reflects judgements about the seriousness of individual breaches of the fundamental protection of human life. Murder is regarded as the most serious, carrying a mandatory life sentence. Other offences carry discretionary sentences of varying severity: manslaughter; causing death by dangerous driving; causing death by careless driving while under the influence of alcohol or drugs; assisting suicide, infanticide; and child destruction. Termination of pregnancy is also illegal, although the Abortion Act 1967 provides defences for doctors that make it lawful in specified circumstances.

Nor does the recognition of the sanctity of human life lead to English law regarding the principle as absolute and inviolable. It is now clear that patient autonomy prevails over the principle that life should be preserved. The crime of attempting suicide was abolished by the Suicide Act 1961. Competent patients are entitled to refuse treatment even if the consequence is that they will die when their life could have been preserved.[2] Further, the courts have accepted that there are circumstances in which health professionals are not obliged to keep patients alive. Where responsible professional judgement finds that it is not in a patient's interest for a particular life-sustaining treatment to be given, then it may lawfully be withheld.[3] There have also been cases in which the courts, required to decide what is best for a patient, have themselves concluded that some treatments should not be given even though the anticipated consequence would be the earlier death of the patient.[4] None of these exceptions to the absolute value of life have permitted the deliberate taking of life in the alleged interests of a patient.

It is also clear that the law recognizes that the obligations of health professionals who care for the dying are not limited to questions of the length of life. One early formulation noted that 'If the first purpose of medicine – the restoration of health – could no longer be achieved, there was still much for the doctor to do, and he was entitled to do all that was proper and necessary to relieve pain and suffering . . .'[5] In more recent decisions, the focus has been on formulations of the doctor's fundamental duty in terms of promoting the patients' best interests, recognizing that this requires consideration of their quality of life as well as the possibility of curative treatment.[6]

To see how this framework affects the question of euthanasia, it is necessary to discuss some of the homicide offences, and some of the defences available to them, in more detail.

Murder

Murder is a common law offence that has been partly codified by statute. The language used to define the offence remains archaic. It is committed when a person unlawfully kills a 'reasonable person in being' with 'malice aforethought'. Four aspects of that definition require consideration. The first is the concept of killing. The courts have held that it is murder to shorten life, even for a few minutes.[7] It is as much murder to kill someone just before they die as it is when they are fully fit.

Second, the word 'unlawful' merely means unjustified. Judicial killing (capital punishment) is no longer a justification. The law does not recognize the belief that a person would be better off dead as a justification for killing them.[8] Proposals to introduce a special defence of mercy killing, based on such a belief, have been rejected.[9]

The phrase 'reasonable person in being' uses the word 'reasonable' to describe humanity rather than the capacity to reason. It covers a child from the point that he or she has an existence independent of the mother and will continue to cover a person up until the point of their death even if they become comatose or otherwise unable to express their views or interact with others. Patients in persistent vegetative state are not regarded as dead by the law. Although the courts have accepted the concept of brain stem death as developed by the medical profession as a legal definition of death,[10] this would not relax the application of murder to euthanasia cases.

Malice aforethought is present where the killer intended to kill or do serious harm to their victim. A person will be taken to have had this intention if they foresee that this will virtually certainly be the consequence of their actions. They do not need to wish that death should occur and motive is not relevant. This comparatively simple current formulation belies a complex history to the concept of intention to murder. However, it makes it clear that the deliberate ending of a patient's life through administration of drugs or other medical means would constitute intentional killing. The special circumstances of pain-killing drugs are considered further below. The main issue in relation to the killer's state of mind concerns the distinction between murder and manslaughter.

Manslaughter

The offence of manslaughter covers unlawful killings where the killer's actions are intentional but 'malice aforethought' is not present. The sentence for manslaughter is discretionary and can range from an absolute discharge to life imprisonment. Most 'mercy killings' that reach the courts do so as prosecutions for manslaughter.[11] There are at least five circumstances in which unlawful killing will amount to manslaughter.

(i) What would be murder but for the existence of provocation. To be sufficient to reduce a charge of murder to that of manslaughter the provocation must have made the accused lose their self-control (a subjective test). However, the law also applies an objective test, requiring the jury to consider whether the provocation would have caused a reasonable person to lose their self-control. Only if both the subjective and objective tests were satisfied would manslaughter rather than murder be committed. There is no limit as to what can constitute provocation. In one case it was found that the persistent crying of a baby could do so.[12] In principle, therefore, observation of a person in extreme suffering could constitute provocation. However, it is unlikely that it could be said that this leads to medical euthanasia being classified as manslaughter. Few juries would believe that a health professional, trained to deal with such matters, would lose self-control in the face of pain.

(ii)   What would be murder but for the statutory defence of diminished responsibility under the Homicide Act 1957. The defence can be raised on medical evidence that the accused suffered from an abnormality of mind. This has been accepted in cases of reactive depression or extreme distress or grief that causes hysterical dissociation. Mercy killings may sometimes be treated as manslaughter by reason of diminished responsibility resulting from distress at the position in which the 'victim' was placed.

(iii) The survivor of a suicide pact, having killed the other party, is guilty of manslaughter rather than murder by virtue of the Homicide Act 1957 section 4 (as amended).

(iv)   Where there is no intention to kill or cause serious harm but death is caused by an unlawful and dangerous act. This is a form of what is known as involuntary manslaughter.

(v)   Killing by gross negligence. In health care cases, the courts have suggested that gross negligence arises where there is such disregard for the life and safety of others when giving care as to deserve punishment.[13]

Defences to homicide

It is not appropriate to explore the whole range of legal defences in this chapter. However, there are some that are important to the debate over euthanasia.

The fact that the accused was not personally and directly responsible for the death does not provide them with a defence. Anyone who is a party to a course of conduct is fully responsible in law. Those who aid, abet, counsel or procure a crime are liable to prosecution. Thus, it is immaterial which member of a health care team administers a fatal injection. All those party to the decision to do so could be charged with homicide. The meaning of aiding, abetting, procuring and counselling is considered below under the heading of suicide.

It is no defence to say that the accused did not intend the consequences of their actions if they knew that death would occur in the ordinary course of events.

Insanity is only a defence where the accused was labouring under a disease of the mind so as not to know the nature and quality of his actions or failed to appreciate that they were wrong. Issues of provocation and diminished responsibility, discussed above, are far more likely to be relevant to euthanasia cases than insanity.

Consent of the 'victim' provides no defence to a charge of homicide or causing serious bodily harm.

In some areas of health care law there is a defence of necessity to enable the best interests of patients to be pursued. Thus it may be lawful to operate on an unconscious person without consent (which would normally be both a civil wrong and a crime).[14] However, while this may justify withholding treatment (see below) it would not permit active killing.

The defence of duress, which is not available for murder, can only be claimed where there is a threat to life. Thus, emotional pressure arising from a patient's distress cannot be said to provide duress absolving a mercy killer's guilt.

The use of pain relief that incidentally shortens life

Despite the rules (i) that people intend the normal consequences of their actions, (ii) that shortening life is killing, and (iii) that there are no special rules for doctors, it appears that the courts have created special rules relating to pain-relieving drugs. In *R v Adams*[15] the court accepted that doctors could administer pain-relieving drugs that they knew might incidentally shorten the lives of the patients. The rationale behind the direction to the jury in the Adams case was that if restoration of health was no longer possible the doctor should do all that was proper and necessary to relieve pain and suffering.

There are probably three tests that have to be satisfied before the defence is available. The patient must be terminally ill, so that the main cause of death is the illness not the treatment. The medication used must be 'right and proper treatment', probably as judged by medical experts. Finally, the doctor's purpose in prescribing the medication must be to relieve pain rather than shorten life. As a matter of legal principle, it is exceptional that such a primary purpose or motive rule is made available, but it now seems well established in the context of palliative care at the end of life.

Infanticide and child destruction

The offences of infanticide and child destruction are unlikely to be relevant to discussion of euthanasia due to the limited scope of the offences, which were created to deal with particular historical legal problems that are now substantially superseded. Under the Infanticide Act 1938 a woman who wilfully kills her child (by act or omission) under the age of twelve months and whose mind is disturbed by not having recovered from the effects of giving birth or lactating is guilty of infanticide rather than murder. Child destruction is an offence committed when a child 'capable of being born alive' is killed before it has an existence independent of its mother.[16] A doctor who carries out a termination of pregnancy within the Abortion Act 1967 is not guilty of child destruction.

Suicide

Prior to 1961, English law reflected the strong condemnation of suicide within the Christian tradition. Committing suicide was a crime and consequently attempting to do so was also criminal, as law necessarily proscribes attempting a criminal act. These offences were abolished by the Suicide Act 1961. Two important issues are raised by this abolition concerning the rights and duties of health professionals in the face of a patient wishing to die. The first is whether they should interfere with such a wish so as to prevent it being carried through. The second is whether patients may seek professional assistance in committing suicide.

In respect of the first issue, it is now clear that it is wrong forcibly to treat a competent patient who refuses treatment in the hope that they will die.[17] Doctors may be able to justify interfering with a suicide attempt by showing that the patient did not actually have the capacity to decide to die. They can reasonably expect that the courts will be sympathetic to those who are reluctant to believe that the person attempting suicide had really thought it through and intended to die. However, it is clear that in principle suicide can be a rational decision requiring respect. The older view that the principle of sanctity of life permitted force-feeding and restraint of suicides is no longer acceptable where the person concerned is found to be competent to choose to die. It should be noted that there might be some circumstances when the mental health legislation might permit compulsory treatment.

The second issue has been addressed specifically in the offence of aiding, abetting, counselling or procuring another person to commit or attempt suicide. This offence, usually known as 'assisting suicide', was created by the Suicide Act 1961 in order to prevent other people being drawn in to a suicide attempt. In the *Bland* decision, the House of Lords made it clear that respecting a person's refusal of treatment would not constitute assisting suicide.[18] Nor would giving people information that they could use to end their life unless suicide was actually encouraged.[19] However, giving medication to a patient saying that it should be taken in order to end their life would overstep the line.[20] Consequently, physician-assisted suicide, even where the doctor takes no active steps in the act of killing (leaving that to the patient), would be illegal under English law.

Selecting the appropriate treatment

The final area of law that requires consideration is that concerning decisions about what treatment is appropriate. The limits provided by the rules on active killing have already been discussed. Selecting treatment options in relation to those who might die if the wrong decisions are made also raises important legal issues about the value placed on human life.

The decision in the *Bland* case examined the law in cases where doctors are accused of failing to sustain life when they could have done so.[21] Interpreted strictly, it held that the test to be applied was whether responsible medical opinion accepted that it was proper to withhold the treatment in question. If such a body of opinion supported withholding the treatment it would not matter that other doctors thought differently. However, many doctors and lawyers have felt it prudent to bring cases to court to seek further guidance on such an important issue. The pattern of decisions indicates that each situation needs individual consideration. The courts have not found it appropriate to take decisions in advance because changes in the circumstances might point to different conclusions. Nor have they found it acceptable to take decisions on whether a person's situation is so dire that they should be permitted to die. Rather they have accepted that some treatments seem too invasive, with too poor prospects of success, to be pursued while (for the same patient) other treatments should be maintained. Thus it may be that antibiotics should be administered to protect against opportunistic infections but artificial ventilation would be too much.

The matter remains, therefore, primarily one for professional ethics rather than law. However, the law indicates that in selecting treatment the continuation of life is an important valuable that should not be sacrificed without good reason in the patient's interests. It also shows that quality of life is not the only relevant factor. For the same person a particular quality of life may be too poor to merit giving one treatment while another should go ahead because it is less intrusive or surer of success.

Euthanasia

We are now in a position to look at the attitude of the law towards euthanasia, in the sense in which we are now using the term as being the equivalent of active killing.

We have seen that the general attitude of the law towards the killing of a human being is that it is usually a crime, though one of varying gravity according to the circumstances. We have seen, however, that it is no longer a crime to kill oneself. But it is still a crime to kill someone else, even at his request, and it is still a crime to help him to kill himself.

It follows that, as the law now stands, save for the rare occasions already mentioned, one cannot put a person out of this world without committing a crime. The doctor cannot, even at the patient's request, administer the lethal dose without committing a crime. He can, however, ease his passage by giving pain-killing drugs.

Should the law be altered so as to admit of more occasions on which it is permissible to kill? It is a question which raises both practical and moral problems.

It would, of course, be comparatively simple to amend still further the law relating to suicide and murder, so that it would no longer be an offence either to assist another to commit suicide or to kill another at that other's request. It would be comparatively simple, but many people think it would be highly dangerous, so dangerous that it is unlikely to be seriously proposed save under severe limitations. The limitations so far suggested are that the right to kill should be limited to the medical profession, and then only in compliance with a well-attested request made by a patient who, when he made it, was fully in possession of his faculties.

It is to be noted that such legislation would leave unresolved the dilemma of the doctor attending the victim of a road accident who appears to be profoundly unconscious with an apparently irreparable injury to his brain. It might actually embarrass the doctor who at present in terminal cases uses a wide discretion based on compassion in the giving of analgesics and the withholding of antibiotics.[22] The probabilities are that, at least initially, only a small number of persons will sign a request for euthanasia, but if such a request should by law become a possibility, the doctor concerned with a patient who has not signed such a request may, by reason of its absence, be more inhibited about exercising his clinical discretion.

Another serious consideration, to which we have already referred,[23] is the effect which such legislation could have on the relationship between doctor and patient. Today there is a large measure of confidence in the medical profession on the part of patients and their relatives. It is generally (and rightly) thought that doctors do not kill. Even so, it is not unknown for patients and their relatives to be suspicious of 'the syringe', lest it be the instrument of killing rather than of alleviation. If in future the law is going to allow doctors to kill, even though under strictly circumscribed conditions, the effect for many will be a disastrous blow to the confidence which they at present have in their medical attendants. A Bill to authorize euthanasia, while it might bring comfort to a sophisticated few, could well bring unease of mind to a much larger number of more ordinary patients and their relations. Were such a Bill again to be introduced and should it display any prospect of being passed into law, it might be wise to insist on the inclusion of a clause excluding from its scope any practitioner in therapeutic practice and confining the right to administer euthanasia to a limited number of persons who are at the same time excluded from therapeutic practice. Although such a clause would in no way meet the objections to euthanasia based on moral principles, it would relieve the patient from the fear, however unjustified, that his medical attendant was likely to kill him.

There are still parts of the world where medical facilities are not readily available and where physical suffering can be both acute and prolonged. Such parts of the world pose their own problems, both legal and ethical. They are not, however, our immediate concern. We are concerned with proposals for legislation for England and Wales, and here the control of pain which medical techniques have now achieved is so great that the occasions are rare on which the resort to killing can alone avoid suffering. Nor can they be sufficiently precisely catalogued for the purposes of legislation, even if to do so were desirable and ethically permissible. The attempt to do so could easily weaken the respect for life which the present law helps to inculcate. Even if it be conceded that in ethics there are occasions untouched by the present law when it may be justifiable to kill, the rarity of such occasions is such that in England and Wales any attempt to legislate for them is almost sure to fail, while the evils to which such an attempt could give rise are so great that the attempt should not be made.

7

Conclusions

1. In its narrow current sense, euthanasia implies killing, and it is misleading to extend it to cover decisions not to preserve life by artificial means when it would be better for the patient to be allowed to die. Such decisions, coupled with a determination to give the patient as good a death as possible, may be quite legitimate.[1]

2. Nor should it be used to cover the giving of drugs for the relief of pain and other distress in cases where there is a risk that they may marginally shorten the patient's life. This too we think legitimate.

3. We have not examined and therefore have not advanced any conclusion about cases where children are born with severely crippling and incurable defects, or where an attempted cure might, if unsuccessful, leave the patient with such a defect. Our concern has been with *voluntary* euthanasia.

4. If all the care of the dying were up to the standards of the best, there would be few cases in which there was even a *prima facie* argument for euthanasia; better alternative means of alleviating distress would almost always be available if modern techniques and human understanding and care of the patient were universally practised.

5. It should be the aim to improve the care of the dying in hospitals and hospices and in their homes to as near this standard as the money and the staff available will allow. We think that, at present, ignorance and mistaken ideas are a greater obstacle than shortage of money or staff.

6. In situations in which, for any reason, the techniques referred to in 4 above are not available (as might happen, for example, in the jungle, in emergencies and accidents, or in war, where medical aid is lacking or insufficient) exceptional cases could conceivably arise in which deliberate killing would be morally justified as being in the best interest of the person concerned.

7.   However, to justify a change in the law in this country to permit euthanasia, it would be necessary to show that such a change would remove greater evils than it would cause. We do not believe that such a justification can be given; for

(a) such cases are very few, and would be fewer still if medical, and in particular hospital, practices were sounder;

(b) a change in the law would reduce the incentive to improve these practices;

(c) the legalization of euthanasia would place some terminal, and even some non-terminal, patients under pressure to allow themselves to be put away – a pressure which they should be spared;

(d) it would also, in practice, be likely to result in recourse to euthanasia in many cases in which it was far from morally justified, and performed for unsound reasons;

(e) in the rare cases (if such there are) in which it can be justified morally, it is better for medical men to do all that is necessary to ensure peaceful dying, and to rely on the flexibilities in the administration of the law which even now exist, than to legalize euthanasia (which would have to be subject to rigid formalities and safeguards) for general use;

(f) although there may be some patients whose relationship with their doctor would not suffer, we believe that for the great majority of patients their confidence in doctors would be gravely weakened.

The Relief of Pain in Terminal Illness

Statistics from records of a hospice which admitted 577 patients in one year

1.   Pain was not a problem for 228 patients. Eighteen of these patients subsequently complained of pain: all had good relief.

2.   349 (63 per cent) patients had pain problems. All but seven patients obtained good relief from their pain. Details of these patients are as follows:

	Sex	Age	Primary Site	Survival (days)	Details
1.	F	58	?Rectum or Ovary	43	Admitted from hospital with intractable burning pain in abdomen, left leg and left perineal area. Seen several times by psychiatrist. Prescribed anxiolytic and anti-depressant drugs. Continued to say the pain was worse than ever up to three days before her death when she slept for most of the time. Said on two occasions she wanted to die to end the suffering. On Diconal for first 11 days. Diamorphine from sixth day. Oral/IM 2.5 -10mg.
2.	F	68	Sarcomatosis ?Uterus	83	Rectal pain radiating down to left leg. Pain controlled after multiple dose adjustments but returned two weeks before death. Further adjustments made: patient died peacefully. Oral diamorphine 10-15 mg. IM diamorphine 10-60 mg.
3.	M	49	Malignant Ascites Unknown primary	8	Pain controlled on Mist. diamorphine 10 mg until day before admission. Easier following paracentesis but increased as abdomen became distended again. IM diamorphine 5-15 mg.

	Sex	Age	Primary Site	Survival (days)	Details
4.	M	26	Disseminated thymoma	122	Secondaries in right shoulder girdle, left scapula and right sacro-iliac joint. Required increasing analgesia. Developed chest pain. Severe pain persisted from time to time. Had phenol block but little change. Oral diamorphine 15-90 mg. IM diamorphine 60-90 mg.
5.	M	76	Pancreas	27	Pain controlled while under care of O.P. staff for three months. Four days before death had haematuria and considerable abdominal pain at times. Oral/IM diamorphine 2.5-10 mg.
6.	M	65	Prostate	5	Bony metastases. Under care of O.P. staff for four months. Flitting pains in body and limbs at and after admission. Pain not fully controlled. Acute episode of pain just before final deterioration. Oral/IM diamorphine 10-20 mg.
7.	M	60	Maxilla	13	Secondaries in neck with extensive local spread: admitted because of severe pain round left eye and abscess in neck. Intermittent severe pain and distress. Up and about until lapsing into coma two days before death. Oral/IM diamorphine 10-60 mg.

In addition 5 patients continued to have pain when moved and 2 when dressings were changed.

Notes

Three of these patients were in the hospice for less than 2 weeks.

Case 4 had difficult social problems and his complaint of pain was often related to these.

Case 1, the only one who wished to die, had a considerable psychological element to her pain.

All received relief while being sleepy but resisted this. None had pain which was impossible to suppress under all circumstances.

HISTOGRAM OF MAXIMUM DOSES GIVEN

Of 577 patients admitted to a hospice during one year 509 required diamorphine to control their pain.

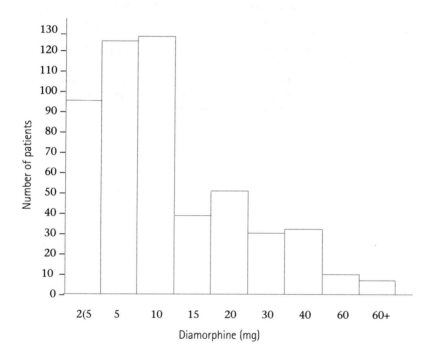

The doses required to achieve relief are shown in this diagram. The number who needed large doses is seen to be small.

Comment by Henry McQuay, Professor of Pain Relief – December 1999

The information in Appendix 1 was collected over 20 years ago, and palliative care has developed considerably since then, but similar details would emerge from an audit done now. The number of cases with pain that is difficult to control would be about the same, and the histogram of maximum doses given would look very similar, as analgesia is still, typically, given in regular, small doses.

In a very small number of cases (7 out of 349 in the data given here) there was pain which was difficult to control. The common causes of such pain are severe pain on movement or pain due to nerve involvement, both of which may be complicated by extreme anxiety and distress. The treatment of such cases has developed considerably since the time of the study. Oral morphine (or methadone) would be used rather than oral diamorphine, although diamorphine is still given by injection because of its solubility; radiotherapy is commonly used for bone pain; and there are effective adjustment drugs for both nerve and bone pain.

Appendix 2

A Joint Submission from the Church Of England House of Bishops and the Roman Catholic Bishops' Conference of England and Wales to the House of Lords Select Committee on Medical Ethics

Foundations

1. The arguments presented in this submission grow out of our belief that God himself has given to humankind the gift of life. As such, it is to be revered and cherished.

2. Christian beliefs about the special nature and value of human life lie at the root of the Western Christian humanist tradition, which remains greatly influential in shaping the values held by many in our society. They are also shared in whole or in part by other faith communities.

3. All human beings are to be valued, irrespective of age, sex, race, religion, social status or their potential for achievement.

4. Those who become vulnerable through illness or disability deserve special care and protection. Adherence to this principle provides a fundamental test as to what constitutes a civilized society.

5. The whole of humankind is the recipient of God's gift of life. It is to be received with gratitude and used responsibly. Human beings each have their own distinct identities but these are formed by and take their place within complex networks of relationships. All decisions about individual lives bear upon others with whom we live in community.

6. For this reason, the law relating to euthanasia is not simply concerned either with private morality or with utilitarian approaches. On this issue there can be no moral or ethical pluralism. A positive choice has to be made by society in favour of protecting the interests of its vulnerable members even if this means limiting the freedom of others to determine their end.

The sanctity of life and the right to personal autonomy

7. Attention is often drawn to the apparent conflict between the importance placed by Christians on the special character of human life as God-given and thus deserving of special protection, and the insistence by some on their right to determine when their lives should end.

8. This contrast can be falsely presented. Neither of our Churches insists that a dying or seriously ill person should be kept alive by all possible means for as long as possible. On the other hand we do not believe that the right to personal autonomy is absolute. It is valid only when it recognizes other moral values, especially the respect due to human life as such, whether someone else's or one's own.

9. We do not accept that the right to personal autonomy requires any change in the law in order to allow euthanasia.

10. The exercise of personal autonomy necessarily has to be limited in order that human beings may live together in reasonable harmony. Such limitation may have to be defined by law. While at present people may exercise their right to refuse treatment (although this may be overridden in special but strictly limited circumstances), the law forbids a right to die at a time of their own choosing. The consequences which could flow from a change in the law on voluntary euthanasia would outweigh the benefits to be gained from more rigid adherence to the notion of personal autonomy. But in any case we believe (para 6) that respect for the life of a vulnerable person is the overriding principle.

11. The right of personal autonomy cannot demand action on the part of another. Patients cannot and should not be able to demand that doctors collaborate in bringing about their deaths, which is intrinsically illegal or wrong.

12. It would be difficult to be sure that requests for euthanasia were truly voluntary and settled, even if safeguards were built into the legislation, and not the result either of depression or of undue pressure from other people. Circumstances may be envisaged in which a doctor managing scarce resources might, perhaps unwittingly, bring undue pressure to bear on a patient to request voluntary euthanasia. Similarly families anxious to relinquish the burden of caring (or to achieve financial gain) might exert influence. Experience suggests that legislative change can lead to significant changes in social attitudes, and that such changes can quickly

extend into supporting actions which were not envisaged by the legislature.

The distinction between killing and letting die

13. Because human life is a gift from God to be preserved and cherished, the deliberate taking of human life is prohibited except in self-defence or the legitimate defence of others. Therefore, both Churches are resolutely opposed to the legalization of euthanasia even though it may be put forward as a means of relieving suffering, shortening the anguish of families or friends, or saving scarce resources.

14. There is a distinction between deliberate killing and the shortening of life through the administration of pain-killing drugs. There is a proper and fundamental ethical distinction which cannot be ignored between that which is intended and that which is foreseen but unintended. For example, the administration of morphine is intended to relieve pain. The consequent shortening of life is foreseen but unintended. If safer drugs were available, they would be used: pain would be controlled and life would not be shortened.

15. Doctors do not have an overriding obligation to prolong life by all available means. The *Declaration on Euthanasia* in 1980 by the Sacred Congregation for the Doctrine of the Faith proposes the notion that treatment for a dying patient should be 'proportionate' to the therapeutic effect to be expected, and should not be disproportionately painful, intrusive, risky, or costly, in the circumstances. Treatment may therefore be withheld or withdrawn. This is an area requiring fine judgement. Such decisions should be made collaboratively and by more than one medically qualified person. They should be guided by the principle that a pattern of care should never be adopted with the intention, purpose or aim of terminating the life or bringing about the death of a patient. Death, if it ensues, will have resulted from the underlying condition which required medical intervention, not as a direct consequence of the decision to withhold or withdraw treatment. It is possible however to envisage cases where withholding or withdrawing treatment might be morally equivalent to murder.

16. The recent judgement in the House of Lords to permit the withdrawal of artificial nutrition and hydration from the PVS patient, Tony Bland, must not be used as an argument for the existing law to be

changed. As with the general question of proportionate means, the complexity of the issue of artificial nutrition and hydration and the associated medical regimes means that there can be no blanket permission as regards PVS patients or those in a similar situation. At the very least, every person's needs and rights must be dealt with on a case to case basis.

The extent of the doctor's duty of care

17. The preceding paragraphs have touched on limits to treatment. The value attaching to human life implies that the primary duties of doctors are to ensure that patients are as free from pain as possible, that they are given such information as they and their carers request and require to make choices about their future lives, and that they are supported through the personal challenges which face them. We believe that to accede to requests for voluntary euthanasia would result in a breakdown of trust between doctors and their patients. Medical treatment might come to be regarded by the vulnerable person as potentially life-threatening rather than something which confers benefit.

The treatment of patients who cannot express their own wishes

18. Where formerly competent people have expressed their wishes about the way they would like to be treated, these should form an important consideration for doctors in determining how to proceed. Such wishes can only act as guidelines since medical conditions may exist for which they are inappropriate. If such wishes are unknown or inappropriate, or if a person has never been competent to express such wishes, then decisions about treatment should be worked out between doctors, families, carers and other health service personnel such as social workers or hospital chaplains.

Advance directives

19. Advance directives may be useful as a means of enabling discussion between doctors and patients about future treatment. Where they exist, they can only be advisory. They should not contain requests for action which is outside the law, nor ask for the cessation of artificial nutrition and hydration. Care should be taken to establish that any advance directive was not made under duress. We would resist the legal enforcement of such directives since the medical conditions envisaged might be susceptible to new treat-

ment, and medical judgements would have to be made about whether a person's condition was such as to require their advance directive to take effect.

Care of terminally ill people

20.   The hospice movement developed from the concern of Christians that people should be helped to die with dignity. This work has enriched not only the lives of terminally ill people but also their carers, volunteers, and health professionals, who have found that caring for those who are dying can be a great source of blessing.

21.   We are concerned that the lessons learned in hospices about pain control and emotional and spiritual support should be applied throughout the health service to all dying people. This requires that medical personnel remain aware of how advice on pain control may be obtained, and that adequate resources are made available for the care of sick and elderly people.

22.   We believe that deliberately to kill a dying person would be to reject them. Our duty is to be with them, to offer appropriate physical, emotional and spiritual help in their anxiety and depression, and to communicate through our presence and care that they are supported by their fellow human beings and the divine presence.

July 1993

Bibliography

J. Agate, 'Ethical considerations: how far does one go?' in *Modern Medical Treatment*, H. Miller and R. Hall (eds), Blackwell, Oxford, 1975.

J. Aitken-Swan, 'Nursing the late cancer patient at home', *Practitioner*, 183, 1959.

S. Amulree, 'James Mackenzie and the future of medicine', *Journal of the Royal College of General Practitioners*, 17, 1969.

J. N. D. Anderson, *Morality, Law and Grace*, Tyndale Press, Cambridge, 1972.

K. Barth, *Church Dogmatics*, T & T Clarke, Edinburgh, 1936–69, III/iv, pp. 397–470.

M. Battin, *The Least-Worst Death: Essays in Bioethics at the End of Life*, Oxford University Press, New York, 1994.

British Medical Association, *Withholding and Withdrawing Life-prolonging Medical Treatment: Guidance for Decision-making*, BMJ Books, London, 1999.

B. Brody, *Suicide and Euthanasia*, Kluwer Academic Press, Dordrecht, Holland, 1989.

J. Burtchaell, *The Giving and Taking of Life*, University of Notre Dame, Ohio, 1989.

A. Cartwright, L. Hockey and J. L. Anderson, *Life Before Death*, Routledge & Kegan Paul, London and Boston, 1973.

Church Information Office, *Ought Suicide to be a Crime?*, London, 1959.

Church Information Office, *Decisions about Life and Death*, London, 1965.

R v Newton and Stungo (1958) *Criminal Law Review* 469

Criminal Law Revision Committee, *Offences against the Person*, HMSO, London, 1980, Cmnd. 7844

Re A [1992] Med LR 303

Re C [1998] 1 FCR 1

Re F [1990] 2 AC 1

Re J [1990] 3 All ER 930

Re J.T. [1998] 1 FLR 48

R v Adams [1957] Crim. LR 365, 773

R v Adomako [1994] 2 All ER 79

R v Arthur [1981] 12 BMLR 1

R v Bourne [1938] 3 All ER 615

R v Bourne [1939] 1 KB 687

R v Charleson [1955] 1 All ER 859

R v Cox [1992] 12 BMLR 38

R v Doughty [1986] 83 Cr App R 319

R v Kemp [1956] 3 All ER 249

R v McShane [1977] 66 Cr App 97

Department of Health and Social Security, *Care of the Dying*, Proceedings of a National Symposium held on 29th November 1972, HMSO, London.

D. Doyle, G.W.C. Hanks and N. MacDonald (eds), *The Oxford Textbook of Palliative Medicine*, 2nd edition, Oxford University Press, Oxford, 1998.

T. F. Fox, 'Purposes of medicine', *Lancet*, 2, 1965.

G. Gorer, *Death, Grief and Mourning in Contemporary Britain*, Cresset Press, London, 1965.

L. Gormally (ed.), *Euthanasia, Clinical Practice and the Law*, Hackett, London, 1994.

Government Response to the Report of the Select Committee on Medical Ethics CM2553, HMSO, London, 1994.

R. Hare, *Personality and Science: an interdisciplinary discussion*, CIBA Foundation, 1971.

F. D. Hart, *The Treatment of Chronic Pain*, Medical & Technical Publishing Co., London, 1974.

J. Hinton, *Dying*, Penguin Books, Harmondsworth, 1967.

J. Hinton, 'Talking with people about to die', *British Medical Journal*, 3, 1974.

W. R. Inge, *Christian Ethics and Moral Problems*, Hodder & Stoughton, London, 1930.

John Paul II, *Evangelium Vitae*, Catholic Truth Society, London, 1995, pp. 115ff.

F. M. Kamm, *Morality, Mortality*, Oxford University Press, New York, 1994.

J. Keown (ed.), *Euthanasia Examined*, Cambridge University Press, Cambridge, 1995.

E. Kubler-Ross, *On Death and Dying*, Tavistock, London, 1970.

H. Kuhse, *The Sanctity of Life, Doctrine in Medicine: A Critique*, Oxford University Press, New York, 1987.

R. Lamerton, *Care of the Dying*, Priory Press, London, 1973.

S. Lammers and A. Verhey, *On Moral Medicine*, 2nd edition, William B. Eerdmans, Grand Rapids, Michigan, 1998,Chs. 6, 14 and 15.

D. R. Laurence, *Clinical Pharmacology*, Churchill Livingstone, Edinburgh, 1997.

Lord Chancellor's Department, *Who Decides? Making decisions on behalf of mentally handicapped adults*, HMSO, London, 1997.

Marie Curie Memorial Foundation, *Report on a National Survey Concerning Patients with Cancer Nursed at Home*, London, 1952.

G. Meilaender, *Bioethics: A Primer for Christians*, William B. Eerdmans, Grand Rapids, Michigan, 1996.

C. M. Parkes, 'The first year of bereavement', *Psychiatry*, 33, 1970.

C. M. Parkes, 'The patient's right to know', *Proceedings of the Royal Society of Medicine*, 66, 1973.

C. M. Parkes, 'Home or hospital? Terminal care as seen by surviving spouses', *Journal of the Royal College of General Practitioners*, 28, 1978.

Parliamentary Debates (House of Lords), 103, cols. 466-506; 169, cols. 552-98.

R. S. Pilcher, Valedictory Address on his retirement from the Professorship of Surgery at University College Hospital Medical School, 1967.

P. Ramsey, *The Patient as Person*, Yale University Press, New Haven, CT, 1970.

W. D. Rees, 'The distress of dying', *British Medical Journal*, 3, 1972.

Report of the Select Committee on Medical Ethics, House of Lords Paper 21-I, HMSO, London, 1994.

Royal College of Physicians Working Group, 'The permanent vegetative state', *Journal of the Royal College of Physicians of London*, 30, 1996.

C. M. Saunders, 'Treatment of intractable pain in terminal cancer', *Proceedings of the Royal Society of Medicine*, 56, 1963.

C. M. Saunders, 'The symptomatic treatment of incurable malignant disease', *Prescriber's Journal*, 4, 1964.

C. M. Saunders, 'Terminal Care', in K. D. Bagshawe (ed.), *Medical Oncology* Blackwell, Oxford, 1975.

P. Singer, *Rethinking Life and Death*, Oxford University Press, New York, 1994.

B. Steinbock and A. Norcross (eds), *Killing and Letting Die*, 2nd edition, Fordham University Press, New York, 1994.

P. Teilhard de Chardin, *Le Milieu Divin*, Collins, London, 1960.

R. G. Twycross, 'Clinical experience with diamorphine in advanced malignant disease', *International Journal of Clinical Pharmacology, Therapy and Toxicology*, 9, 1974.

P. J. van der Maas, J. J. M. van Delden and L. Pijnenborg, *Euthanasia and other Medical Decisions*, Elsevier, Amsterdam, 1992.

R. Veatch, *Death, Dying and the Biological Revolution*, 2nd edition, Yale University Press, New Haven, CT, 1989.

Voluntary Euthanasia Society, *A Plea for Legislation to Permit Voluntary Euthanasia*, London, 1970.

E. Wilkes, 'Terminal cancer at home', *Lancet*, 1, 1965.

J. Wilkinson, *Christian Ethics in Health Care*, Handsel Press, Edinburgh, 1998.

G. Williams, *The Sanctity of Life and the Criminal Law*, Faber & Faber, London, 1958.

Zbigniew Zylicz, 'The story behind the blank spot', *The American Journal of Hospice and Palliative Care*, July/August, 1993.

Legal Cases

AG v Able [1984] 1 All ER 277

Airedale NHS Trust v Bland [1993] 1 All ER 821

R v Windle [1952] QB 826

Secretary of State for Home Office v Robb [1995] 1 All ER 677

Notes

Twenty-five years on: Introduction to the Second Edition

[1] P. J. van der Maas, J. J. M. van Delden, and L. Pijnenborg, *Euthanasia and other Medical Decisions concerning the End of Life*, An investigation performed on the request of the Commission of Inquiry into the Medical Practice concerning Euthanasia, Health Policy Monographs, **22/1 & 2** Special Issue, Elsevier, Amsterdam, 1992.

[2] Zbigniew Zylicz, 'The story behind the blank spot', *The American Journal of Hospice and Palliative Care*, July/August, 1993, pp. 30–34.

[3] A. Cartwright, L. Hockey, and J. L. Anderson, *Life Before Death*, Routledge & Kegan Paul, London and Boston, 1973.

[4] The case examples quoted in this essay are all personally known to the author. No further identifying details are given in order to preserve patient confidentiality.

[5] R. Hare, *Personality and Science: an interdisciplinary discussion*, CIBA Foundation, 1971, p. 92.

[6] House of Lords, *Report of the Select Committee on Medical Ethics* (HL Paper 21-1), London, HMSO, 1994.

[7] Lord Walton of Detchant in *Hansard* (House of Lords) 9th May 1994, 554: 83 col. 1344ff.

[8] British Medical Association, *Advance Statements about Medical Ttreatment*, BMJ Books, London, 1995 (see especially pp. 6 and 15).

[9] Lord Chancellor's Department, *Who Decides? Making decisions on behalf of mentally handicapped adults*, HMSO, London, 1997.

[10] Working group convened by the Royal College of Physicians, 'The permanent vegetative state', *Journal of the Royal College of Physicians of London*, 30, 1996, pp. 119–21.

[11] PVS is usually understood to mean 'persistent vegetative state'. The Royal College of Physicians used the term 'permanent vegetative state' in order to define the condition more precisely.

Preface to the First Edition

[12] J.Wilkinson, *Christian Ethics in Health Care*, Handsel Press, Edinburgh, 1998.

[13] The first half of this chapter has now been substantially updated by Jonathan Montgomery.

Chapter 2: Moral Considerations

[1] In 1950 the House of Lords debated a motion in favour of the principle of voluntary euthanasia, but it was withdrawn without a division. (Parliamentary Debates (House of Lords), 169, cols. 552–98).

² For an account of discussions at the time see Glanville Williams, *The Sanctity of Life and the Criminal Law*, Faber, London, 1958, pp. 297ff.

³ Parliamentary Debates (House of Lords), 103, cols. 466–506.

⁴ See *Decisions about Life and Death*, Church Information Office, 1965. Case history C on p. 2 is one example.

⁵ See Paul Ramsey, *The Patient as Person*, Yale University Press, New Haven, CT, 1970, Ch. 3.

⁶ *A Plea for Legislation to Permit Voluntary Euthanasia*, Voluntary Euthanasia Society, 1970, p. 13.

⁷ See Chapter 5 for a fuller development of this point.

⁸ See Chapters 4 and 5.

⁹ Cf. *A Plea for Legislation to permit Voluntary Euthanasia*, p. 19.

Chapter 3: Theological Considerations

¹ J. N. D. Anderson: *Morality, Law and Grace*, Tyndale Press, Cambridge, 1972.

² Job 1.21.

³ See above, p. 8.

⁴ See above, pp. 10–11.

⁵ Church Information Office, *Ought Suicide to be a Crime?*, London, 1959, p. 28.

⁶ P. Teilhard de Chardin, *Le Milieu Divin*, Collins, London, 1960, pp. 69ff.

⁷ W. R. Inge, *Christian Ethics and Moral Problems*, Hodder & Stoughton, London, 1930, p. 373.

⁸ Matthew 7.12.

⁹ Matthew 22.39.

¹⁰ See above, p.10–11.

Chapter 4: Case Histories Discussed

¹ p. 29.

² Information about the incidence of pain is provided in Appendix 1.

³ C. M. Parkes, 'The patient's right to know', *Proceedings of the Royal Society of Medicine*, 66, 1973, p. 537.

⁴ C. M. Parkes, 'The first year of bereavement', *Psychiatry*, 33, 1970, p. 444.

⁵ See Chapter 2 above, p.5.

Chapter 5: Further Medical Considerations

¹ S. Amulree, 'James Mackenzie and the future of medicine', *Journal of the Royal College of General Practitioners*, 17, 1969, p. 3; T. F. Fox, 'Purposes of Medicine', Lancet, 2, 1965, p. 801; R. S. Pilcher, Valedictory Address on his retirement from the Professorship of Surgery at University College Hospital Medical School, 1967.

² J. Agate, 'Ethical Considerations: how far does one go?' in *Modern Medical*

Treatment, H. Miller and R. Hall (eds), Blackwell, Oxford, 1975.

[3] J. Agate, personal communication, 1974.

[4] J. Agate, 'Ethical Considerations: how far does one go?'.

[5] A. Cartwright, L. Hockey and J. L. Anderson, *Life Before Death,* Routledge & Kegan Paul, London and Boston, 1973.

[6] J. Aitken-Swan, 'Nursing the late cancer patient at home', *Practitioner,* 183, 1959, p. 64; Marie Curie Memorial Foundation, *Report on a National Survey concerning patients with cancer nursed at home,* 1952; W. D. Rees, 'The distress of dying', *British Medical Journal,* 3, 1972, p. 105; E. Wilkes, 'Terminal cancer at home', *Lancet,* 1, 1965, p. 799.

[7] *Life Before Death,* p. 222.

[8] Department of Health and Social Security, *Care of the Dying,* Proceedings of a National Symposium held on 29th November 1972, HMSO, London, 1973.

[9] C. M. Parkes, 'Home or hospital? Terminal care as seen by surviving spouses', *Journal of the Royal College of General Practitioners,* 28, 1978, pp. 19–30.

[10] See above, Chapter 2, p. 5, esp. pp. 13–14..

[11] C. M. Parkes, personal communication, 1974.

[12] G. Gorer, *Death, Grief and Mourning in Contemporary Britain,* Cresset Press, London, 1965.

[13] A. Cartwright et al., *Life Before Death,* p. 228.

[14] J. Hinton, *Dying,* Penguin Books, Harmondsworth, 1967; R. Lamerton, *Care of the Dying,* Priory Press, London, 1973; E. Kübler-Ross, *On Death and Dying,* Tavistock, London, 1970; C. M. Saunders, 'Treatment of intractable pain in terminal cancer', *Proceedings of the Royal Society of Medicine,* 56, 1963, p. 191; C. M. Saunders, 'The symptomatic treatment of incurable malignant disease', *Prescriber's Journal,* 4, 1964, p. 68; C. M. Saunders, 'Terminal Care', in K. D. Bagshawe (ed.) *Medical Oncology,* , Blackwell, Oxford, 1975.

[15] F. D. Hart, *The Treatment of Chronic Pain,* Medical & Technical Publishing Co., London, 1974.

[16] D. R. Laurence, *Clinical Pharmacology,* Churchill Livingstone, Edinburgh, 1997.

[17] R. G. Twycross, 'Clinical experience with diamorphine in advanced malignant disease', *International Journal of Clinical Pharmacology, Therapy and Toxicology,* 9, 1974, p. 184.

[18] C. M. Parkes, 'The first year of bereavement', *Psychiatry,* 33, 1970, p. 444.

[19] J. Hinton, 'Talking with people about to die', *British Medical Journal,* 3, 1974, p. 25.

Chapter 6: Legal Considerations

[1] Article 2.

[2] *Airedale NHS Trust v Bland* [1993] 1 All ER 821.

[3] *Ibid.*

[4] *E.g. Re J* [1990] 3 All ER 930; *Re C* [1998] 1 FCR 1.

[5] *R v Adams* [1957] Crim LR 365, 773.

[6] *Airedale NHS Trust v Bland* [1993] 1 All ER 821.

[7] *R v Adams* [1957] Crim LR 365; *R v Arthur* [1981] 12 BMLR 1; *R v Cox* [1992] 12 BMLR 38.

[8] *Airedale NHS Trust v Bland* [1993] 1 All ER 821, 890.

[9] Criminal Law Revision Committee, *Offences Against the Person*, HMSO, London, 1980, Cmnd. 7844.

[10] *Re A* [1992] Med LR 303.

[11] Report of the Select Committee on Medical Ethics, Oral Evidence, HL Paper (1993–4), 28–II, 18, 25.

[12] *R v Doughty* [1986] 83 Cr App R 319.

[13] *R v Adomako* [1994] 2 All ER 79.

[14] *Re F* [1990] 2 AC 1.

[15] [1957] Crim LR 365 followed in *R v Arthur* [1981] 12 BMLR 1 and *R v Cox* [1992] 12 BMLR 38.

[16] Infant Life (Preservation) Act 1929.

[17] *Secretary of State for Home Office v Robb* [1995] 1 All ER 677. The point was also made by the members of the House of Lords in *Airedale NHS Trust v Bland* [1993] 1 All ER 821, although it was not strictly relevant on the facts.

[18] *Airedale NHS Trust v Bland* [1993] 1 All ER 821, 866.

[19] *AG v Able* [1984] 1 All ER 277.

[20] *R v McShane* [1977] 66 Cr App 97.

[21] *Airedale NHS Trust v Bland* [1993] 1 All ER 821.

[22] See the discussion of Case history 7 above, p.41–43.

[23] See above, pp.14 and 42.

Chapter 7: Conclusions

[1] See Church Information Office, *Decisions about Life and Death*, London, 1965.

Index